The Walter Lynwood Fleming Lectures
in Southern History

New South—New Law

The Legal Foundations of
Credit and Labor Relations in the
Postbellum Agricultural South

Harold D. Woodman

Louisiana State University Press
Baton Rouge and London

Copyright © 1995 by Louisiana State University Press
All rights reserved
Manufactured in the United States of America
First printing
04 03 02 01 00 99 98 97 96 95   5 4 3 2 1

Designer: Glynnis Phoebe
Typeface: Granjon
Typesetter: Moran Printing, Inc.
Printer and binder: Thomson-Shore, Inc.

Library of Congress Cataloging-in-Publication Data
Woodman, Harold D.
    New South, new law : the legal foundations of credit and labor relations in the postbellum agricultural South / Harold D. Woodman.
    p. cm. — (The Walter Lynwood Fleming lectures in southern history)
    Includes bibliographical references and index.
    ISBN 0-8071-1941-5 (cloth : alk. paper)
    1. Agricultural laws and legislation—Southern States—History—19th century. 2. Farm tenancy—Southern States—History—19th century. 3. Agricultural laborers—Legal status, laws, etc.—Southern States—History—19th century. 4. Agricultural credit—Law and legislation—Southern States—History—19th century. 5. Liens—Southern States—History—19th century. I. Title. II. Series.
KF1682.W66   1995
343.73'076—dc20
[347.30376]
                                                                94-31543
                                                                    CIP

The paper in this book meets the guidelines for permanence and durability of the Committee on Production Guidelines for Book Longevity of the Council on Library Resources. ∞

For Leonora

Contents

Acknowledgments ix

Introduction 1

CHAPTER ONE
"For the Encouragement of Agriculture"
The Origins of the Crop Lien Laws 5

CHAPTER TWO
"To Regulate the Law of Liens"
The Evolution of the Crop Lien Laws 28

CHAPTER THREE
"An Obvious Distinction Between a Cropper and a Tenant"
The Legal Status of Landlords, Croppers, and Tenants 67

CHAPTER FOUR
"The Important Business of Farming with Hired Labor"
Law and Postbellum Southern Society 95

Cases Cited 117

Index 123

Acknowledgments

The essays in this book were originally delivered in a slightly different and abbreviated form as the Walter Lynwood Fleming Lectures at Louisiana State University in April, 1990. I am honored by the invitation to deliver the lectures and appreciate the warm hospitality Karl A. Roider, Jr., and his colleagues in the LSU History Department extended during my stay in Baton Rouge. A special thanks is due Gaines Foster, who met me when I arrived, hosted a magnificent reception for me at his home, introduced me in a most flattering way at one of my lectures, and delivered me to the airport at an unseemly early hour in time for my trip home.

I benefited from a number of discussions after each lecture. Especially helpful were conversations with Richard H. Kilbourne, Jr., a Clinton, Louisiana, attorney and legal scholar. Mr. Kilbourne kindly sent me a copy of his book, *Louisiana Commercial Law*, which I read with great profit.

I am delighted to acknowledge the help I received from several institutions. I undertook part of the research for this study while a fellow at the National Humanities Center in the Research Triangle in North Carolina; I wrote an early draft of the original lectures while serving as a Senior Research Scientist at the University of Michigan in Ann Arbor; and the generous leave policy of Purdue University provided me with the time necessary to complete the research and writing. The results of my preliminary investigations of some of the matters discussed in this book originally appeared in *Agricultural History*: 53 (January, 1979), 319–37; 56 (January, 1982), 215–30. I am grateful to that journal for permission to use parts of this material in this study. Tracking down the various laws and cases took me to a number of law libraries where librarians cheerfully met my requests for materials that their usual patrons seldom need and use. Especially helpful were the law libraries and librarians at the University of North Carolina, Chapel Hill; Yale University; and the Library of Congress.

At this point, most "acknowledgments" contain long lists of colleagues and friends who read and commented on early drafts of the manuscript. Unlike most, however, I have not circulated the manuscript widely, but two prepublication readers deserve my warm acknowledgment. I have been especially fortunate that my editor has been Margaret Dalrymple, the Assistant Director and Editor-in-Chief of Louisiana State University Press. Like all good editors, she corrected my mistakes, pointed out obscure and sometimes incorrect formulations and quotations, and suggested changes that improved the manuscript.

The other prepublication reader was Lester H. Cohen, a dear friend and former colleague. Les, who taught intellectual history for more than a decade at Purdue University and is now a practicing attorney in Indianapolis, carefully read the manuscript and offered valuable criticisms and suggestions from the dual perspective of a fine historian and a skilled attorney. He saved me from many errors, explained legal obscurities that I had not recognized and understood, and helped me refine some of my conclusions—all of which improved the manuscript. I shall always be grateful for his help and for his warm enthusiasm for what I had done.

My greatest debt is to Leonora. She didn't live to see this book, but her influence is in it and in everything else I have written or, for that matter, shall write in the future. She is physically gone, but during our long marriage I gained so much from her critical intelligence and her love that she remains indelibly a part of me and my work.

New South—New Law

Introduction

This book deals with very familiar institutions. Anyone with even a passing knowledge of the history of the United States knows something about crop liens, tenancy, and sharecropping in the postbellum South. General textbooks all discuss them, as do all histories of the postbellum South. Indeed, in histories of southern agriculture, of the alliance movement, and of populism, lien laws, tenancy, and sharecropping are usually central to the discussion. It is surprising, therefore, that given their importance, there is no general history of crop lien laws in the South nor of the evolution of the laws relating to sharecropping and tenancy. This book is an attempt to provide some of that history.

My work is designed to do more than fill in some missing details. My research on the history of postemancipation southern agriculture has convinced me that the lack of a full understanding of the origins and evolution of the laws relating to liens, sharecropping, and tenancy has resulted in serious misunderstandings of the social and economic history of the postbellum South. Too often historians have seen the lien laws as part of a merchant conspiracy that forced former slaves into a slavelike social system, led to increasing tenancy among whites, and locked the South into almost a century of grinding poverty and economic stagnation. By failing to see the intent of the authors of the original lien laws and the changes in the laws, along with the reasons for the changes, and by failing to see and appreciate the significance of the differences between tenancy and sharecropping in law and in practice, some present a picture of postbellum southern agriculture that is at once monolithic and unchanging except for growing misery and poverty. I hope that the essays that follow, by providing the missing details, will help to clear up some of these misunderstandings. I hope also that the essays will make a modest contribution to the ongoing discussion and debate concerning the relationship between law and social change; my thoughts on this important question appear as the final chapter.

The laws discussed in the following pages raise no great constitutional principles enunciated by the United States Supreme Court or by famous judges. Indeed, only a few of the cases discussed ever reached the federal courts; these were the peonage cases, about which there was little to debate in the highest court, and in any event, peonage, although reprehensible when it appeared, was not a central feature of postbellum southern agriculture. The statutes and court cases discussed here were local, involving for the most part contracts dealing with labor, tenancy, and credit; and the actors—litigants, legislators, and judges—were minor, local figures whose names have been forgotten by most historians. But the laws were an important part of the revolution that ended slavery and created a free labor system in the postemancipation South.

Because my discussion seeks to outline the evolution of the law supporting the new free labor system and because it traces changes in the formal law—that is, legislation and court decisions—it reveals only part of the story, providing only a glimpse into the day-to-day workings of that system as presented in the evidence that surfaced in the disputes that reached the courts.[1] Only a few disputes ever reached the courts, and fewer still reached the appellate courts that are major sources for this study. Most disagreements undoubtedly ended in an informal settlement outside the courtroom in the absence of the niceties of formal litigation. This is hardly surprising given the unequal distribution of power, wealth, and education in the postbellum South.[2]

1. I am at work on a longer study of postbellum southern agriculture that will attempt to describe and analyze in greater detail the practices associated with the legal changes discussed here.
2. Even today, in instances where both parties have adequate resources and knowledge, their attorneys settle most legal disputes without recourse to litigation. When one side lacks such resources and knowledge or the ability to interest pro bono representation, "settlement" occurs by default. This undoubtedly happened regularly in disputes between wealthy landowners or merchants and poor farmers, tenants, and croppers. However, as we shall

I am well aware that there is not a one-to-one relationship between law and practice. Some laws are openly flouted because penalties are slight, rarely assessed, or nonexistent. Unenforced laws or laws enforced in ways that do violence to their letter and spirit have far different effects from those vigorously and rigorously enforced, and the effects are different still when the laws are not uniformly enforced. Access to the law requires information and entails expense; a law that provides protection, redress of grievances, or particular rights has little meaning to someone who is ignorant of the law's provisions or is unable to pay legal fees.

Equally important is the existence of what may be called informal law—rules, regulations, and customs that allow settlement of differences without recourse to formal law, the legislature, and the courts. This informal law may be "legal" in that it covers matters that the formal law accepts or upon which it is silent, or it may be illegal because legislation and the courts have declared it so, but unless civil or criminal proceedings are undertaken, the formal law becomes irrelevant. Finally, and probably most important, the informal law may have no real legal standing at all because it is more or less accepted practice and has not caused the controversy that would induce either the legislatures or the courts to intervene, or because those who might seek to change such practices lack the resources, financial and organizational, to do so.

Nevertheless, the formal law discussed in the following pages is of great importance because it provided the basic legal structure for the development of the free labor system in the postbellum South. Emancipation radically altered economic and class relations in the South. It abruptly ended the legal contradictions in slave law as well as the legal conflicts between North and South stemming from differing property relations.[3] But if abolition made

---

see, in some disputes that did reach the higher courts, the poor did get legal representation. More commonly, however, in most of the litigation, although a cropper or tenant would be named in the case, the real issues involved disputes between parties that could afford legal counsel.

3. See Mark Tushnet, *The American Law of Slavery, 1810–1860: Considerations of Humanity and Interest* (Princeton, 1981); Edward Lynn Ayers, *Vengeance and Justice: Crime and Punishment in the 19th-Century American South* (New York, 1984); Michael Stephen Hindus, *Prison and Plantation: Crime, Justice, and Authority in Massachusetts and South Carolina, 1767–1878* (Chapel Hill, 1980); Eugene D. Genovese, *Roll, Jordan, Roll: The World the Slaves Made* (New York, 1974), 25–49; Elizabeth Fox-Genovese and Eugene D. Genovese, *Fruits of Merchant Capital: Slavery and Bourgeois Property in the Rise and Expansion of Capitalism*

the law concerning slave property relations irrelevant, it did not automatically produce a full body of law to replace that which had been destroyed, or, to put it in more general terms, emancipation destroyed the slave social system without automatically creating a new free labor system in its place. If planters and farmers who had depended upon slave labor were to get their lands cultivated in the postemancipation era, they had to offer wages and working conditions that would entice the labor they needed. Former slaves now had the right to choose their employers and to demand what they considered to be adequate wages and working conditions, or to withhold their labor.

Besides depriving slaveowners of their ability to command a labor force, emancipation deprived them of their most important form of wealth and therefore their most important source of security for the credit they needed to return to production. The state legislatures sought to solve this problem by enacting the crop lien laws, but in doing so they inadvertently created new problems that added to the difficulties of developing a free labor system.

Inevitably, new problems and efforts to solve them produced conflicts that the legislatures and the courts sought to resolve. The new free labor and credit systems that emerged operated within the boundaries the formal law established. This study attempts to describe the development of those boundaries.

(New York, 1983), 337–87; Paul Finkelman, *An Imperfect Union: Slavery, Federalism, and Comity* (Chapel Hill, 1981).

CHAPTER ONE

"For the Encouragement of Agriculture"
The Origins of the Crop Lien Laws

On February 18, 1867, the governor of Mississippi gave his approval to a new law entitled "An Act for the Encouragement of Agriculture." The particular encouragement offered by this law and by similar legislation passed in most of the other southern states during 1866 and 1867 was the crop lien. The laws stipulated that anyone who provided supplies, or money to purchase supplies, necessary to produce a crop received a lien on that crop when gathered.[1]

Southern farmers and reformers would later condemn the lien laws as a major source of the region's agricultural woes—overproduction, low prices, debt peonage, and rising tenancy. Historians have tended to agree. The lien system, C. Vann Woodward has written, "represented one of the strangest contractual relationships in the history of finance" and constituted "a curse to the soil." But the Mississippi legislators, like the authors of the first lien laws in the other southern states, did not consider the system their legislation sought to establish to be strange, and they were convinced that the new laws would indeed encourage agriculture. They certainly did not en-

---

1. Alabama, *Acts, 1865–66* (Jan. 15, 1866), 44; Florida, *Acts, 1866* (Jan. 13, 1866), 61–62; Georgia, *Acts, 1866* (Dec. 15, 1866), 141; Louisiana, *Acts, 1867* (March 28, 1867), 351; Mississippi, *Laws 1866–67* (Feb. 18, 1867), 569–72; North Carolina, *Public Laws, 1866–67* (March 1, 1867), 3–4; South Carolina, *Acts, 1866* (Sept. 20, 1866), 380–81; Texas, *Acts, 1866* (Oct. 27, 1866), 64. Arkansas and Tennessee did not pass new lien laws. Borrowers in these states relied upon existing laws that allowed them to mortgage a crop to be grown.

vision that the laws would cause landowners to lose their farms or that they might support merchants at the expense of farmers. On the contrary, the conservative planter-dominated legislatures that enacted the first lien laws were convinced that the legislation would solve the problems faced by the agricultural South in the wake of a devastating war and the emancipation of the slaves.[2]

The most immediate, pressing, and obvious economic problem following the defeat of the Confederacy was the need to rebuild the region's agricultural economy and feed its population. On this all could agree. But disagreement surfaced immediately over what rebuilding the agricultural economy entailed. What seemed obvious to most whites, victors and defeated alike, was to return to the production of the South's money crops with the former slaves as the primary work force on the larger farms. But this was a goal that most former slaves did not share. Their desire for land of their own, as expressed in the slogan "forty acres and a mule," reflected their desire to escape from the slavelike work regimes associated with staple crop production and to achieve independence from their former masters. Understandably enough, former slaves found little meaning in a freedom that required them to work for their former owners pretty much as they had as slaves, receiving as wages just enough to buy food, shelter, and clothing; and they did not find convincing the argument of northerners that such was the condition of free workers elsewhere in the nation. The refusal to distribute land to former slaves closed that particular avenue to their achieving independence from their former owners, but it did not end their desire for such independence, which they sought to achieve by other means.

Even as the issues of land distribution and labor regimes were being worked out, farmers needed credit to buy seed and equipment to plant a crop and, for the larger producers, food and other supplies to provide to workers. Wartime devastation and neglect and limited available savings increased the need to borrow in order to return to peacetime production, but these same conditions—to say nothing of the loss of slave property—meant that borrowers had little security to offer potential lenders.

2. C. Vann Woodward, *Origins of the New South, 1877–1913* (Baton Rouge, 1951), 180. Except in Virginia, the first crop lien laws were all enacted by governments elected under the Johnsonian reconstruction policies, that is, before Congress imposed its "radical" policies. Virginia is an exception only in timing; when the state passed its first lien law in 1873, the legislature was safely in the control of the planters and their supporters. Virginia, *Acts, 1872–73* (April 2, 1873), 357–58.

With the new lien laws, the conservative southern legislators sought to establish a credit system for the region's farmers based upon traditional, and therefore familiar, arrangements, but adjusted to new conditions. It would also be a system that the planter-authors of the laws expected would finance a return to commercial production using free labor organized and managed along prewar lines. Such was the original intent of the authors of the lien laws. But the laws' authors soon discovered that the new laws created new problems that threatened to undermine the goals they sought.

Conservative southern lawmakers realized that to encourage agricultural production it was necessary, as the title of the North Carolina law put it, "to secure advances for agricultural purposes." Farmers needed equipment, seed, food, clothing, and other supplies in order to grow crops. Because emancipation, depressed land values, and extensive property losses arising from war and neglect deprived most farmers of resources that could serve as security for loans, they needed a new source of security to induce potential lenders to supply the funds necessary for production. The crop lien would provide the absent security by giving lenders special rights to the crops to be grown in the future with the supplies or money they advanced. Farmers lacking enough personal or real property to back needed loans could borrow by pledging the forthcoming crop as security.

The lien laws were not a completely unknown or untried innovation. On the contrary, they merely provided a legal basis for what had been largely a traditional relationship between farmers and lenders before the Civil War. Antebellum planters had regularly received advances in supplies, consumer goods, and even cash from their commission merchants (or factors, as they were usually called) with the understanding—sometimes explicit, but usually merely implicit—that they would send their produce to the merchants, who would then find a buyer.[3] The merchants would deduct from the proceeds of the sale the cost of any advances along with interest, a service charge, and any other expenses incurred in handling and selling the crop for the planter.

Antebellum courts had ruled that a factor who advanced money, supplies, and other goods to planters had a lien on their crops, but the courts declared that lien to be very limited, covering only those advances that actu-

---

3. Although all factors offered much the same services to their customers, they tended to specialize in one of the crops they handled: rice, tobacco, sugar, and cotton.

ally went toward producing a crop, not personal and household goods and other services that factors regularly supplied their customers. Furthermore, the lien came into force only when the factor actually received the crop to sell, and in the absence of a written agreement that the planter would send his crop to the factor—the typical situation—the factor had no legal guarantee that he would receive it and thereby get his lien.

Nevertheless, factors felt secure in making their loans. The word of a gentleman was enough to induce the factor to make requested advances; he was confident that he would receive enough of the crop to cover advances even without a written guarantee, and should the planter send all or part of his crop to someone else, the factor who had made the loan remained confident that he would be paid. Of course, he knew also that borrowers had ample resources in land, equipment, and, most important, slaves to cover any outstanding debts should ordinary recourse to the civil courts be required to collect on a loan. In practice, factors seldom resorted to litigation to collect a debt. Indeed, so confident were the factors in their customers' promises and resources, they would regularly carry over a debt from one year to the next without requiring any kind of written agreement. Small farmers, who usually did not deal directly with factors, received the same services from local merchants and storekeepers, who in turn dealt with the factors on much the same terms as did the planters.[4]

The authors of the first lien laws simply sought to replace traditional practices with more specific safeguards to solve the new postwar problems. The word of a gentleman had far less meaning when the gentleman's land and equipment had fallen in value, his slaves had disappeared, and the free labor supply seemed so uncertain. The legislators assumed that by providing legal security in a future crop, they would solve the credit problem and enable farmers to return to production on pretty much the same basis as before the war. They were aware, of course, that emancipation meant more than the loss of wealth and the credit it commanded, that it meant also the loss of control over the work force. The same legislatures that passed the first lien laws also enacted the black codes designed to establish the control over blacks that emancipation had destroyed.

If the black codes indicated how the planters thought free black labor

---

4. Harold D. Woodman, *King Cotton and His Retainers: Financing and Marketing the Cotton Crop of the South, 1800–1925* (Lexington, 1968), 5–125. On the country storekeepers, see Lewis E. Atherton, *The Southern Country Store, 1800–1860* (Baton Rouge, 1942).

should be controlled, the lien laws indicated how they expected postemancipation agriculture would be organized. A closer look at the first Mississippi law clearly reveals their thinking. Section 1 provided that debts "contracted for" supplies "necessary for the cultivation of a farm or plantation, shall constitute a prior lien upon the crop of cotton." Written in the passive voice, the section did not indicate who would do the contracting, but the legislators assumed that the contractors would be owners or renters who, if they did not do all the work themselves, would hire laborers. This becomes obvious in section 2, which granted a second kind of lien. By shifting to the active voice, the lawmakers made it very clear who was involved and how they envisioned the future of postemancipation agriculture:

> ... when any owner or lessee of any plantation or farm, shall make any contract with laborers to cultivate such farm or plantation for a share or shares of a crop, in lieu of wages, and such owner or lessee shall make advances of money, provisions or clothing, in accordance with such contract, such owners or lessees shall have a lien on the share of such laborers for the payment of the same.

Section 8 of the law dealt with rent. Apparently assuming that tenants would be those who rented entire plantations or farms and satisfied that landowners who leased their lands already had adequate legal protection, the authors of the legislation did not include a lien for rent but instead simply stipulated that the law in no way interfered with "any of the rights or remedies now allowed by law of the landlord for rents due or owing for any plantation or farm."[5]

Thus, the Mississippi legislators, believing that "the encouragement of agriculture" depended upon the ability of the state's farmers to get credit, enacted the crop lien law. If farmers hired workers who were to receive their wages in the form of a share of the crop produced—a common practice—and if the planters then advanced food, clothing, or money to their workers during the year, they received guarantees of repayment by another lien, this one on the wages of the workers, that is, on the share of the crop the workers would eventually receive. Clearly, the legislation rested upon the assumption that former slaves would become wage workers laboring under the direction of their former masters. Although free, the workers, coerced

5. Mississippi, *Laws, 1866–67,* 569–72.

by the lack of alternative opportunities and by the stringent black codes, would remain deeply dependent upon their employers. Because they would not be paid until the crops were gathered, workers had to remain at work for the entire year or lose their wages; and because they needed food and clothing during the year, long before receiving their wages, they had to get such goods on credit from their employers at prices and interest rates determined by the employers. In short, the law would help farmers to get the credit they needed while at the same time providing them with a large measure of control over their employees.

Such was the vision of the conservative authors of the lien laws. But reality turned out to be quite different. Not only did the radicals in Washington destroy the planned social control set out in the black codes, but the planters discovered that the lien laws themselves could endanger their income and weaken their ability to control their labor force. Ironically, in seeking solutions to the credit and labor control problems the planters' representatives in the Johnsonian reconstruction legislatures had enacted laws that could—and did—create unforeseen new problems that undermined the very purposes of the laws.

Borrowers and lenders alike quickly discovered that the new lien laws, along with existing laws and the developing free labor system, could create multiple, competing claims against the same crop. Because the laws specifically designated the crop to be grown as security for loans, anyone who at the end of the season would have a crop or even a portion of a crop he had grown had the security to borrow. This meant that a propertyless farmer who rented a farm would have that security. It also meant that a worker whose pay would be a portion of what he produced had security for a loan. Thus, the same crop could be encumbered for rent, supplies advanced, and wages, and when that crop could not satisfy all the claims against it, conflict arose over whose claims would be satisfied.

The potential for competing claims for rent and supplies became the most immediate and obvious problem. If a landless farmer rented land and then borrowed money or bought supplies on credit to enable him to cultivate it, both the landowner and the lender became his creditors, and the relative status of the claims of each could become important if the renter failed to produce enough to pay both. This was a familiar problem, because it had existed before the Civil War, but antebellum renters usually owned slaves and had other resources that lessened the risk for landowners and lenders.

Only in Alabama did the legislators clearly and unambiguously recognize that postemancipation conditions required special legislation to protect the landowner who leased his lands. Alabama had granted landlords liens on their tenants' crops for rent before the Civil War, and this lien for rent remained unchanged in the postwar years. The state's new law giving a lien to anyone providing advances to plant a crop clearly ranked the two liens, stating that the lien for advances "shall have preference of all other liens, except that for the rent of the land on which said crop may be made." This made the landlord's lien for rent superior to that of the supplier, in conformity with existing antebellum law.[6]

In other states the ranking of liens was far less certain. Georgia's first postbellum lien law did not mention liens for rent; it merely provided that those advancing supplies to make a crop could get a lien on the crop for the supplies advanced.[7] Perhaps the legislators believed it unnecessary to include liens for rent because antebellum Georgia law, which remained in force, granted the landlord a lien on the crop for rent. In any event, neither the old nor the new law unambiguously ranked the two possible liens. When a controversy over lien priority reached the Georgia court in 1869, it ruled that the lien for rent was "superior to all other liens."[8] But this decision was a narrow ruling that settled the particular case before the court and, as we shall see in the next chapter, left the general question of lien priority unanswered.

If Alabama, explicitly, and Georgia, much less so, protected landlords who leased their plantations and thereby increased the risk of a merchant who advanced supplies to the renter, the reverse was true in Mississippi. Neither the first lien law nor existing law granted Mississippi landlords a lien for rent. Therefore, a supplier who had received a lien became the primary creditor and could take all the proceeds of the crop even if that meant that the landlord would not receive his rent. In a case that reached the Mississippi Supreme Court in 1873, a landlord argued that his providing land to a renter constituted an advance under the law and therefore gave him a lien for his rent. But the court disagreed, ruling that the state's lien law

---

6. *Code of Alabama, 1852*, 465; *Revised Code of Alabama, 1867*, 580, Alabama, *Acts, 1865–66* (Jan. 15, 1866), 44. In a case decided in 1847, the Alabama court ruled that the landlord had a lien for rent and could attach the crop in the hands of a merchant who had received it while rent was still due: Dulany v. Dickerson, 12 Alabama 601 (1847).

7. Georgia, *Acts, 1866* (Dec. 15, 1866), 141.

8. Section 2260, *Georgia Code, 1867*; Toler *et al.* v. Seabrook, 39 Georgia 14 (1869).

of 1867, which granted a lien for supplies, could not be construed to grant a lien to the landlord who supplied the land on which the crop was grown. "We have held in several cases," the court repeated a year later, "that neither at common law, nor under our statute, does the landlord have a lien upon the agricultural products, or the chattels on the premises for rent."[9]

The law in North Carolina seemed to protect the landlord's rent, but it did not grant him a lien on the crop, creating uncertainties that potentially increased the risk of both landowners and merchants. On March 1, 1867, North Carolina enacted its crop lien law, which gave anyone advancing money or supplies a lien on crops grown "in preference to all other liens existing or otherwise." The same legislation also provided that the "lien shall not affect the rights of landlords to their proper share of rents."[10]

These landlords' rights, spelled out in legislation enacted just a day earlier, provided that when a tenant agreed to pay rent in the form of a portion of the crop grown, that portion "shall be deemed the property of such landlord, as fully as if vested in him." Should the landlord believe that the renter intended "to use, sell or destroy" the portion of the crop due for rent, he could "maintain an action of replevin" for his property, that is, he could get a court order to get goods wrongfully taken by others. If the agreement with the tenant provided that rent be paid in cash, the landlord could "attach enough of the crop raised on the land to secure the rent due."[11] Presumably, in passing the two laws in quick succession, the legislators intended that the lien for advances given by a tenant, although superior to all other liens, would not reach that portion of the crop he owed the landlord for rent, inasmuch as the legislation granted the landlord a form of ownership of that portion, even if he did not possess it.

The distinction the legislators made between the superior lien granted anyone who advanced money or supplies to make a crop and the rights of landlords arose from long-standing landlord-tenant law in that state as well as elsewhere in the nation. That law deserves extended attention here because it affects not only these particular North Carolina statutes but also because it becomes an important consideration in later statutes and decisions

---

9. Stewart v. Hollins *et al.*, 47 Mississippi 708 (1873); Arbuckle v. Nelms, 50 Mississippi 556 (1874). As we shall see in the next chapter, Mississippi did not grant a lien for rent until 1876.
10. North Carolina, *Public Laws, 1866–67* (March 1, 1867), 3–4.
11. North Carolina, *Public Laws, 1866–67* (Feb. 28, 1867), 89–90.

elsewhere and becomes a central issue in determining the distinction between tenants and sharecroppers and the different rights and obligations under each tenure form.

Traditional landlord-tenant law gave the tenant possession of the rented property and ownership of the goods produced on the property, subject, of course, to the payment of agreed-upon rent. This gave the tenant independence from landlord interference and provided him with most of the rights of ownership during the period of the lease. The landlord could not interfere with the tenant's work unless he could demonstrate that the tenant's activities endangered the payment of rent to become due or that the tenant was doing damage to the rented property; and the landlord could not take or use the goods produced on the rented property, even when the rent came due.

Subject only to specific conditions set down in the lease, the tenant could use the property as he pleased, and he could dispose of the product and encumber any of his own property, including the product, in a manner he deemed best without landlord interference. The landlord's only legal recourse if the tenant failed to pay the rent was to sue the tenant for breach of the rental contract. This traditional law applied whether the rent was in money or was in the form of a share of the crop grown; the landlord had the right to his share—that is, to his rent—but he did not own that share, nor could he take possession of it until the tenant divided out the portion due the landlord. In short, until the division was made, the landlord had a right to his rent under the rental contract, but the tenant retained legal ownership of the entire product, including that portion which had been promised as rent.

This traditional landlord-tenant relationship had been clearly spelled out in numerous decisions in northern courts before the Civil War[12] and was

12. A Pennsylvania court ruled that the landlord due a share of the crop as rent did not gain title until the tenant divided the crop and delivered the landlord's share to him: Burns v. Cooper, 31 Pennsylvania (7 Casey) 426 (1858). Even if the landlord had possession of a part of the crop that later would be his (that is, after the division), he could not prevent the tenant from taking it: Briggs v. Thompson, 9 Pennsylvania (9 Barr) 338 (1848). Nor could a third party to whom the landlord was indebted take what would later be the landlord's share from the tenant. Until the tenant paid the share, it was not the landlord's property: Ream v. Harnish, 45 Pennsylvania (9 Wright) 376 (1863). A New Jersey court ruled that a tenant paying rent in a share of the crop controlled and possessed the crop and could dispose of it without the landlord's consent; he would, of course, remain responsible for the payment of rent, presumably from the proceeds of the sale: Doremus v. Howard, 23 New Jersey Law

well established in North Carolina. Control of the crop was in the hands of the tenant until it was divided, the North Carolina Supreme Court ruled in 1839, and in the same decision it denied that the landlord had a lien on his tenant's crop for rent.[13] Legislation in 1840 gave the landlord an interest in the crop for his rent, but, the court ruled, that interest did not constitute a lien, nor did it give the landlord ownership or possession before the tenant actually made the division. The landlord was merely one of several possible creditors.[14]

The authors of the postbellum North Carolina law were aware of the traditional law of landlord-tenant relations and of the absence of a landlord's lien for rent in the state; the language stating that the landlord's portion was his property "*as if* vested in him"[15] recognized that the property was in fact not his. Thus, although the North Carolina laws seemed to protect the landlord's rent from his tenants' other creditors, they contained enough ambiguity to raise the potential for conflict between the lien-holding supplier seeking reimbursement for his advances and the landlord seeking his rent, when the crop grown was not large enough to pay both.

But such problems would become painfully obvious only in retrospect when conflicts arose. They did not seem to trouble the authors of the first crop lien laws in North Carolina—and elsewhere in the postbellum South as well. The lawmakers undoubtedly concluded from their antebellum experience that existing law adequately protected landowners who leased

---

(3 Zal.) 390 (1852). In Vermont, a tenant who had agreed to pay half the crops grown as rent removed and consumed the whole of the crop before making a division. The landlord sued the tenant, charging that he had taken the landlord's property, but the court ruled that the landlord had to seek other legal redress because the tenant had not divided the crop, and therefore the landlord did not own his promised share: Hurd v. Darling, 16 Vermont 377 (1844). In Iowa, a court ruled that a landlord who entered his property leased to a tenant to take possession of the share of the crop due him as rent could be sued for trespass; the landlord had no right to his share until the tenant made the division: Blake v. Coats, 3 Greene 548 (Iowa, 1852). In a Michigan case decided in 1864, a tenant mortgaged his growing crop, and when the mortgage holder sought to take possession, the landlord took the crop and refused to release it. The court ruled that the landlord's action was a "conversion," that is, the unlawful taking of another's property: Figuet v. Allison, 12 Michigan 328 (1864).

13. Deaver v. Rice, 20 North Carolina 567 (1839).

14. Peebles v. Lassiter, 33 North Carolina 73 (1850); Ross v. Swaringer *et al.*, 31 North Carolina 481 (1849).

15. Emphasis added.

their plantations and farms. In some states, continuing antebellum law and new legislation provided the landlord with a lien for his rent that was superior to all others.[16] In states without a rent lien law or where legislation failed to rank the landlord's right to his rent and the lien for advances, landlords, like other creditors, had established legal avenues of redress open to them.

In any event, when the legislatures enacted the first postwar lien laws, few landlords expected to lease their lands; they planned to work their lands using gang labor paid in cash or in a share of the crop. Even smaller landowners who had owned only a few slaves envisioned hiring freedmen to work much as they did before emancipation rather than transforming them into tenants. Those who contemplated leasing their lands did not envision dividing their property into small rental tracts to be operated by their former slaves. If plantations were to be leased, the renters would be large-scale operators who would hire freedmen to work in gangs. The immediate and pressing problem for all was to get the credit necessary to secure equipment, workstock, and seed necessary to plant a crop, and the larger planters who either owned or rented plantations needed credit to get the food and clothing they expected to provide as part of their employees' wages. Therefore, guarantees beyond existing law that rent would be paid would seem far less important to the authors of the first postbellum lien laws than the need to provide facilities to induce lenders to supply credit to farmers in the war-devastated South.

Nevertheless, the new laws created an unanticipated potential for conflicts between landowners and merchants with competing claims on a crop to be grown. Adding to the potential for conflicts were still other claims on a future crop. Workers who were to be paid a share of the crop produced, or those who were to receive their wages at the end of the season from the proceeds earned from the sale of the crop, also had a claim.

Of course, if the crop was sufficient to satisfy all claims, no problem would arise. But if the crop could not satisfy all claims, as was often the case in the first few years after the Civil War because of bad weather and a decline of prices from wartime highs, then disputes arose over whose claims took precedence. The degree of protection given landlords, merchants, or workers was the degree to which the risks of the others increased. Compli-

16. Antebellum lien laws for rent existed in some northern states. See, Case v. Hart, 11 Ohio 364 (1842); Esdon v. Colburn, 28 Vermont (2 Williams) 631 (1856).

cating matters even further, at least in the early postemancipation years, was federal law that allowed Freedmen's Bureau agents to intervene. In sum, the new laws generated conflicts that threatened to undermine the very goals that the lien laws were expected to reach.

The nature of these conflicting claims and the effects of efforts to resolve them may best be illustrated by a concrete example.

Late in 1866, W. R. Hunt and Giles L. Driver, the executors of the estate of Eli M. Driver, began planning for the new crop year on the large Driver plantation in the rich delta land of Tunica County, Mississippi. Conditions were hardly propitious. Although the Civil War had been over for more than a year, the political and economic situation in Mississippi—indeed, throughout the South—in late 1866 was confused and uncertain. When President Andrew Johnson issued his Proclamation of Amnesty and Reconstruction in May, 1865, Mississippi and the other former Confederate states promptly amended their constitutions to abolish slavery and repudiate the Confederate debt; each then elected its state officials and its congressional delegations. The Union had been restored, the president told Congress when it met in December.

But Congress disagreed, and refused to seat the South's senators and representatives. The South's selection of so many former Confederates to represent it, the continuing antagonism toward Federal forces in the South, often erupting into violence, and the enactment of the black codes by the new state legislatures outraged a majority in Congress who concluded that southerners had not learned the lesson taught by defeat on the battlefield. Early in 1866 Congress extended the scope of the Freedmen's Bureau, empowering it to intervene in both civil and criminal affairs and to establish military courts to try persons accused of depriving blacks of their civil rights, and then it clearly defined those rights in a Civil Rights Bill. Johnson vetoed both bills only to have his veto overridden. Congressional radicals, their power enhanced by victories in the election of 1866, imposed new restrictions on the southern states and made it clear that Congress, rather than the president, would determine when a state was reconstructed and deemed eligible to reenter the Union.

Hunt and Driver and the other Mississippians with whom they dealt undoubtedly knew that events in Washington would affect their business affairs in Tunica County. As they began planning for the 1867 crop year, they saw congressional radicals enhance their power by victories in the 1866 elections, but they could only guess about what the new Congress would do when it assembled in the spring of 1867.[17] In any event, they could not wait for the establishment of political stability if the Driver lands were to go into production in 1867, and like landowners throughout the South, they sought to make the best arrangements they could under the circumstances. Deciding to lease the plantation rather than run it themselves, the executors of the Driver estate began negotiations with a group calling itself Wing, Cox & Co. By January 1, 1867, the two parties had reached a rental agreement, for on that day Wing, Cox & Co. gave Hunt and Driver their note for $4,000, payable on October 1, 1867. On January 15, 1867, after completing some further negotiations, the two parties took their contracts to the office of the probate clerk of Tunica County to be officially recorded.[18]

Under the terms of the agreement, Hunt and Driver leased the plantation to Wing, Cox & Co. for $4,000 and some other unspecified property for an additional $675. The post-dated notes indicated that Wing, Cox & Co. expected to pay the rent due at the end of the crop year from the proceeds of the crop they would grow on the rented land. To secure their notes—that is, to base them on some tangible asset rather than a simple promise—the renters provided Hunt and Driver with two liens: one on the corn and cotton to be grown on the plantation during the year; the other on the work animals and farm implements that Wing, Cox & Co. would supply for use on the plantation.

The rent negotiations completed, Wing, Cox & Co. hired about forty freedmen, promising some of them cash wages at the end of the season and others wages in the form of a share of the crop to be produced. Wing, Cox & Co. now had the land and the workers but lacked the equipment and supplies they needed to begin production and to feed and house their workers during the year. To fill these needs, they turned to merchants White & Billingsley, who agreed to provide the necessary supplies and equipment on credit. It is unclear from the available evidence whether this agreement with

17. The radicals, of course, would impose new restrictions on the southern states, including black suffrage. As we shall see, the new state governments would enact laws that significantly altered those enacted by the legislatures elected under Johnson's reconstruction.

18. Hunt v. Wing *et al.*, 57 Tennessee 139 (1872). The various agreements and the litigation in the lower courts discussed below are presented in the evidence summarized in the report of this case.

the merchants came before or after the passage of Mississippi's lien law. The evidence merely indicates that the agreement had been made "after" that of the one with the landowner, that is, after January 15; Mississippi's lien law went into force on February 18. In any event, the merchants felt adequately secured by what is called in the evidence a "mortgage" on the crop to be grown and on the equipment they supplied. This mortgage, like the agreements with Hunt and Driver, was duly recorded in the Tunica County courthouse.

Clearly, Wing, Cox & Co. had more confidence in their ability to turn a profit than they had funds to finance their enterprise. There is no evidence that they used any of their own funds. Their whole operation was based upon credit, making the entire crop still to be grown encumbered for rent, for supplies, and for wages.

The credit burden proved too great, for the crops produced could not satisfy all who had claims upon them. Wing, Cox & Co. apparently abandoned any attempt to sort out the various debts they faced at the end of the season. When the $4,000 note came due on October 1, they did not pay it, whereupon Hunt and Driver went to court and received a distress warrant (an order allowing the county sheriff to seize the crops, work animals, and equipment and sell them to satisfy the rent agreement). In November the sheriff sold enough of the cotton, corn, animals, and equipment to pay the $4,000 note and $75 on the other note. Twenty-four bales of cotton produced on the Driver plantation remained in the sheriff's hands, but it was obvious that this was far from enough to pay all the remaining debts: the $600 still due Hunt and Driver, the workers' wages, and the merchants' bill.

The workers, fearing that they would lose their year's wages, turned to the Freedmen's Bureau for aid. The local agent, M. J. Manning, quickly intervened. Acting on the authority granted the bureau by federal law, he bypassed the local court and seized the twenty-four bales of cotton from the Tunica County sheriff and shipped them to a cotton firm in Memphis to be sold, with orders that the proceeds of the sale be used to pay the workers. White & Billingsley, the merchants who had advanced supplies and equipment to Wing, Cox & Co., seeing the last of the crop upon which they had a mortgage for advances disappearing, immediately turned to the Memphis Law Court, where they sought and received a writ of replevin (an order to retrieve property wrongfully seized). Acting on the instructions of the court, the sheriff in Memphis took possession of the cotton when it arrived, preventing delivery to the merchants to whom the bureau agent had sent it, and delivered it instead to another merchant who promptly sold it for $1,200.

At this point, the landowners Hunt and Driver intervened. They returned to court, this time in Tennessee, seeking to prevent the Memphis merchant from giving the $1,200 to White & Billingsley. Arguing that Wing, Cox & Co. still owed them $600 for rent, that their lien predated the mortgage of White & Billingsley, and that White & Billingsley were aware of their earlier lien, they received writs of attachment and injunction, court orders that prevented White & Billingsley from receiving any part of the funds until the issue was settled. They then sued Wing, Cox & Co. for the outstanding $600, claiming that they had to be paid first out of the proceeds of the twenty-four bales.[19]

Before the case could come to trial, however, the Freedmen's Bureau agent once again intervened. This time he sought redress in a local court. Acting as the freedmen's "next friend," a legal procedure allowing one who was not a party to a suit to intervene in another's behalf, Manning filed a suit in the Chancery Court of Memphis, a court of equity, contesting the validity of Hunt and Driver's lien and White & Billingsley's mortgage, but arguing also that even if both were valid, equity would make the right of the workers to their wages superior to both. Therefore, Manning argued, the $1,200 should not go to either until the workers received their wages. Specifically, Manning asked that the court delay its decision in the dispute between the landlord and the merchants until the freedmen's case could be heard and their wages paid. The other parties both objected to the delay, and when the chancery court overruled their objections, thereby siding with Manning, Hunt appealed the ruling to the Tennessee Supreme Court, which finally heard the case in 1872.

In its decision, the supreme court first considered matters of procedure, noting that not only was Manning's case improperly drawn, but also that Manning had no right to sue in the first place. The right to sue for others as a "next friend" was reserved for instances where the proper party to a suit

19. Wing, Cox & Co. were out of the picture, for no matter how the Memphis Law Court ruled, they would receive no part of the remaining $1,200. Procedure required that they be sued because they were the debtors and still the legal owners of the proceeds from the sale of the crop. For the same reason, they would remain defendants in the case in the appeal to the Tennessee Supreme Court.

was under a "disability." Infants, lunatics, idiots, and married women unable to sue in their own names were examples of those under such a disability, the court explained. But the blacks, it insisted, suffered under no such disability; they were "*sui juris*," fully capable of handling their own affairs. "We know," the court intoned, unconsciously revealing a serious disability blacks labored under when dealing with southern judges, "that as a race they are far below the white man in intelligence," but this did not justify Manning acting for them. Apparently enjoying the opportunity to lecture the representatives of the Freedmen's Bureau on the rights of blacks, the court reminded Manning's lawyer that blacks "have all the rights, before the courts of the country, possessed by any other class of citizens." Then, having established the procedural error in Manning's suit, the court nevertheless agreed to consider it, announcing that the blacks' "want of intelligence, and their ignorance of the complicated relations of business life" justified relaxing the rules.

But the court found the substance of the case as erroneous as the procedure. Manning had argued that justice and fairness—that is, equity—provided the workers with a lien on the crop they had produced that was superior to all other liens, even those that "may have been executed prior to their employment as laborers." The court declared this view to be "entirely new and unknown . . . and if it has any foundation whatever we have failed to discover it." It admitted that the argument of the lawyer representing the workers was "ingenious" and "plausible," but so too was the landlord's response:

> It is said that without the labor there can be no crop, and if there is no fruit there can be no profit for the landlord or any one else. This is true, but the landlord replied that without his land, which had caused him so much labor, and the expenditure of so much capital to make it fit for cultivation, the laborers would be without a home and without the means of acquiring bread to sustain life, or give him [*sic*] bone and muscle to perform the labor.

The court declared that it was not empowered to settle the dispute on the basis of such "abstract" claims, however ingenious and plausible they might appear. The court's duty, it declared, was to apply the law, and in this instance the law was clear—the party with the superior lien was the landlord whose paramount right to his rent was well established in common law and in statute, and for good reason, the court explained: "The public good requires that owners of the soil should clear their lands and build houses, and by these improvements not only to beautify and adorn the country and add to its material wealth, but to afford larger facilities for the support of the industrial classes, and the maintenance of a denser population."

This explanation might appear to be as "abstract" as that which the court rejected, but it became concrete and real, at least in the eyes of the Tennessee judges, because it was grounded in the law. In fact, the legal grounds were shaky. Mississippi statutes did not grant the landlord a prior lien for his rent either in 1867 when the case began or even in 1872 when the Tennessee Supreme Court made its ruling.[20]

The court would have had a better argument had it simply noted that the landlords had filed a written agreement that created a lien and that this lien predated the agreements with the workers. But this would not have answered the workers' contention that justice and fairness made their rights to their wages superior to all other claims. The court was obviously seeking a general legal principle to support the landlords' claims for rent as opposed to those of the workers for wages. It "makes no difference," the court ruled, whether Hunt and Driver "have a lien as landlord, or by mortgage on the crop, or by neither." Only if the workers could "show that they, by the laws of Mississippi, or by virtue of some contract, had acquired a lien on the cotton" that was superior to the rights of the other parties could they sustain their case. This they had failed to do.

Of course, the court admitted, "that the laborer's claim for compensation for his labor is a most meritorious one cannot be denied." But however meritorious the workers' claim might be in general, in this case the law did not support it. If the court were to accept Manning's contention that the workers had a lien superior to that of the others, "it would be *jus dare* not *jus dicere*," that is, the court would be making rather than declaring or applying the law. At best, the workers might be considered legitimate creditors with a right to the "surplus of the fund, if there was any," but this is not what Manning argued in his suit. Instead, he insisted that they had a superior lien, but he provided no evidence to support his claim.

The court admitted that those who agreed to work for a share of the crop rather than for cash wages might have a better case, but only if they

20. See, Stewart v. Hollins *et al.*, 47 Mississippi 708 (1873).

could show that their agreement was that their share should come out of the particular twenty-four bales in question. Inasmuch as Manning did not provide such evidence, his case was inadequate. The court then took the opportunity to attack the federal laws that had granted the bureau the legal powers that had precipitated the controversy. In what was surely obiter dictum, inasmuch as the issue was not before the court, it announced that Manning had illegally seized the cotton in the first place, a ruling that in effect declared the federal law under which Manning had acted to be unconstitutional.

The court concluded by reversing and dismissing the ruling of the chancery court, thereby allowing the original case to be heard. Manning was assessed court costs for the litigation in the chancery court and in the appeal to the supreme court. The court added that the freedmen had the right to file another, better suit if they so chose, but the ruling suggested that the workers had little chance to file a proper claim. The court had made it quite clear that the workers did not have a superior lien and could sustain their intervention only by showing that they had a specific agreement giving them a lien on the particular parcels of cotton in the dispute, an agreement they did not have. As a result, the outcome of the litigation in the lower court would determine how the proceeds from the sale of the cotton at issue would be divided between the landlord and the merchants. The court's adamant comments about the rights of the landlord suggested that the proper outcome in the Memphis Law Court would be to pay the landlord the $600 remaining on his lien and give the rest of the money to the merchant. The workers lost their claim for their wages.

The conflicts in this case arose because each debtor had a legal contract[21] that gave him rights that he insisted took precedence over the others in a crop that could not satisfy all. More specifically, the legal questions raised two different but related matters—the kind of encumbrance each of the contracts created and the priority enjoyed by each encumbrance. The landlord, the

21. It will be recalled that evidence in the case indicated that the agreements with the landowners and the merchants were written and recorded in the Tunica County Courthouse. The evidence does not indicate whether the agreements with the workers were written, but at the time, the Freedmen's Bureau encouraged employers and employees to sign written contracts and give a copy to the local agent. Although the report in this case provides no evidence of the existence of a bureau-authorized written contract, the court specifically called the agreement with the workers a "contract."

workers, and the merchants all claimed to have a lien on the future crop: the landlord because of a specific written agreement with his tenant; the workers because of their rights in equity to their wages; the merchants because of a duly executed mortgage. If the Tennessee court was satisfied that it had found enough existing law to settle the particular issues before it, its decision could not provide any lasting precedent to resolve the more general problems that had surfaced in the litigation.

Indeed, the legal basis for the decision was questionable to begin with. Even if the court's cavalier dismissal of the Freedmen's Bureau agent's right to act under federal law is ignored as obiter dictum prompted by political enthusiasm, the ruling that Mississippi statutes gave the landlord a prior lien for his rent was flat wrong. The evidence showed that the landlord had a written and recorded agreement that specifically created a "lien" on the crop that predated the written agreement between the tenant and the merchants that created a "mortgage" on the crop. But if the merchants had made their agreement after February 18, 1867, the date on which Mississippi's first lien law went into effect, they might have argued that their agreement created a "prior" lien for supplies, which, in the absence of a statutory lien for rent, might have put the landlord's lien in jeopardy, even though it predated that of the merchants. Moreover, although the landlord's lien and the merchant's mortgage predated the wage contract with the workers, both these debts could have been in jeopardy had the wage contract with the workers created a lien with priority over both, as the agent of the Freedmen's Bureau contended.

These are not merely hypothetical possibilities. They would arise in litigation throughout the South because the first lien laws designed simply to help farmers get needed credit created considerable ambiguity concerning who could get a lien and of lien priority when several existed. In addition, unanticipated actions by landowners, merchants, and workers soon introduced further complications. If former slaveowners expected the lien laws to provide the credit they needed to return to production with hired labor, the former slaves had a different vision for the future, one that gave more meaning to their newly won freedom than that contemplated by their former owners.

The freedmen, with the support of local merchants, quickly discovered ways to take advantage of the lien laws in order to decrease their dependence upon their employers, a result completely unforeseen by those who wrote the initial laws. If the workers would receive as their wages a portion of the crop at the end of the year, they would therefore have produced a crop on which they could, under the law, give a lien in order to get advances. The laws all stated this explicitly by allowing anyone who advanced supplies necessary to make a crop to get a lien on that crop. The legislators had simply assumed that payments to the workers during the year would come from their employers as advances on their wages; indeed, as we have seen, the Mississippi law specifically gave employers a lien on the workers' pay—that is, on their portion of the crop—to secure such advances. But the freedmen easily found merchants who were willing to grant them goods on credit in return for a lien on their share of the crop being grown, and many borrowed from them rather than from their employers—or, as often happened, from both.

Ironically, then, the lien law, designed to help the planters get credit and maintain control over their work force, became a means for workers to escape dependency upon their employers by providing them with an alternative source of credit. When the freedmen seized their new opportunity, they created new and unforeseen conflicts, which freedmen, planters, and merchants all attempted to resolve in a manner that afforded each the greatest benefit.

The problems arose because of uncertainty concerning the extent of the supplier's lien under the new laws, that is, how much of the production of the farm it covered. The early laws were usually silent on the question because the legislators simply assumed that lenders had a lien on the entire output of the farm and that they would carefully monitor their loans to make sure that they did not lend more than the crop on which they had a lien would yield. This was a reasonable assumption, provided that the borrowers were landowners doing their own work or planters hiring labor, because in either case the borrower would then own the entire crop produced, and therefore the entire crop would be encumbered by the lien. But when planters borrowed from merchants, and when workers, whose promised wages were a share of the crop they produced, also borrowed from merchants, and when planters leased their entire plantations or portions of their lands to others who in turn borrowed, sharp conflicts arose over the extent of the liens. Workers, lessors, planters, and merchants all claimed rights to a gathered crop that was often too small to satisfy their combined claims.[22]

The legal question created by such conflicting claims was lien priority,

22. The conflict was exacerbated during the first three postwar years, when crops were unexpectedly poor, but it continued in later years as prices for the southern staple crops declined.

and most of the early laws failed to establish such priorities. If in some states the landlord's lien for rent was superior to other liens, in others, it will be recalled, the landlord had no lien for rent or there was considerable ambiguity concerning the landlord's rights. The ranking of other liens or rights, such as the workers' right to their wages and the relative standing of two or more liens on a crop, when each was an advance to grow that crop, remained to be determined.

Workers, planters, and merchants did not—indeed, could not—wait for the legislature and the courts to act to solve all the new problems, and the problems increased in complexity as time passed. Planters, pressed by their lien-holding creditors, would sell the crop produced to merchants to satisfy their debt and then refuse to pay the workers, claiming that whatever surplus—if any—remained was rightfully theirs as payment for the land, equipment, and advances they had supplied. Workers, thus deprived of their wages, refused to contract with such employers for the following year, claimed fraud, and sought the aid of the Freedmen's Bureau to collect their wages. When the bureau set up its own courts to adjudicate conflicts and supported the workers' claims to their wages, even to the extent of seizing crops held by planters and merchants in order to force the payment of wages due, it in effect gave workers a lien for their wages that was superior to that of the other lien holders. But when merchants, to satisfy their lien, took a planter's entire crop, including that portion promised as workers' wages, they acted as if their lien took precedence over the amount due the workers as wages. And when merchants took the workers' shares to satisfy their liens, they acted as if merchants' liens were superior to those of planters who also may have advanced supplies to the workers. When the law was silent or ambiguous or varied from state to state and when the Freedmen's Bureau had federal legal authority to intervene and by-pass local courts, resolution of disputes became increasingly difficult.

Planters were caught in a bind. They needed credit and hence the lien laws, but they resented those lenders who used the lien laws to deal directly with the workers, a practice that put the planters' returns at greater risk and diminished their control over their labor force. Attempts to intimidate the offending merchants or to coerce the workers provided little relief as freedmen simply refused to work for those planters who employed such tactics. Some planters, unable or unwilling to cope with the new problems, sought to avoid them by abandoning their attempts to hire gang labor and instead rented small portions of their lands to freedmen, taking as rent a portion of what the renters produced. But this tactic merely compounded the problem of lien priority. The tenants took advances from merchants, and at the end of the season, merchant lenders and landlord lessors often competed for rights to the same crop.

Small farmers were often caught in the same bind. The lien laws allowed them to get the credit they needed, but they quickly discovered that the cost could be high. Merchants would advance supplies and take a lien only on a readily marketable crop, which forced small farmers to increase the proportion of their efforts and land to the growing of staple crops at the expense of food crops. This in turn meant that they had to borrow more in order to get the necessary food for themselves and their workstock. If the small farmers sought to increase their output and income by hiring workers or by renting out those portions of their lands that they and their families could not work themselves, they faced the same problems of lien priority that the planters faced.

I have deliberately posed these problems in legal terms, and indeed, I shall attempt to show how the law eventually did determine who could get a lien, the proper procedure to be followed, and which lien took priority when more than one existed on a single crop. But solving the legal question of lien priority was not a matter of discovering the intent of the legislators who enacted the original lien laws; their intent was clear enough. Nor was resolution of the problems simply a matter of finding appropriate precedents or enacting new laws to clarify existing law, although this is how it would appear in judicial proceedings. Politics, not the law, determined the *manner* in which problems finally got resolved. By defining the rights of employers and workers, borrowers and lenders, and landowners and renters, the legislatures and the courts created the legal support for new social relationships in the postbellum agricultural South. The new law, like the new social relationships, developed in response to the problems generated by the class conflicts arising from efforts to build a free labor society and the changing political arrangements this struggle produced.

Emancipation made significant legal changes inevitable and of immediate concern. But the precise nature of those changes was far from inevitable, and the changes that took place profoundly affected the entire society, not just the freedmen and their former owners. If the outcome seems inevitable when viewed from the end of the story, for the participants the results were neither foreseen nor inevitable. On the contrary, legal changes came piecemeal in response to particular problems as they arose. These piecemeal legal changes did not take place in a political and social vacuum, and they did not have a single foreordained solution. Indeed, the recognition that a problem existed as well as how it might be solved was not primarily a legal matter at all, but rather depended upon how different groups perceived their goals, how they defined the problems that seemed to stand in the way of achieving such goals, and how much political power they could employ to get the law to conform to their interests.

The conservatives who enacted the first lien laws discovered that they had unanticipated and troublesome results, results that became even more troublesome when the radical legislatures that replaced the conservatives enacted new legislation that protected and increased the rights of workers and small-scale tenants and, to a degree, of the merchants with whom they dealt—all at the expense of the large landowners. But in every state, as soon as the redeemers had replaced the radicals, they enacted new legislation that shifted the balance of power to the landowners. One set of new statutes and court rulings increased the power of the landlords at the expense of merchants, tenants, and workers by clarifying and altering the priority of liens, making the landlord's lien for both rent and advances superior to all other liens and mortgages.[23] Other laws increased the power of employers by defining a particular kind of worker, the cropper, and then by sharply limiting the rights of the cropper.

The evolution of the lien laws and of the laws regarding sharecropping is the subject of the next two chapters.

23. In every instance liens for taxes were always superior to all private liens. In my discussion of lien priorities I have ignored the public obligations.

Chapter Two

"To Regulate the Law of Liens"
The Evolution of the Crop Lien Laws

Georgia's first crop lien law, approved on December 15, 1866, was brief, concise, and seemingly unambiguous. It provided that "factors and merchants shall have a lien upon the growing crops of farmers, for provisions furnished and commercial manures furnished, upon such terms as may be agreed upon by the parties."[1] The authors of the Georgia crop lien law, like those who wrote similar laws in other states, sought to create legal security in the form of a crop to be grown in the future so that farmers could get supplies and hire workers to plant crops. Although enacted by the conservative, planter-dominated legislature elected under Johnsonian reconstruction, the law created special problems for the very landowners it was designed to help.

Ironically, one provision in the law, designed, it seems, to give special protection to the landowner, had the opposite effect. Presumably because the legislation gave a lien specifically to "factors and merchants" who advanced supplies, the legislature added another section to the law to give the same protection to landlords who advanced supplies to their tenants: "... landlords may have, by special contract in writing, a lien upon the crops of their tenants, for such stock, farming utensils and provisions furnished such tenants for the purpose of making their crops." Thus the law protected both merchants and landlords who advanced supplies by giving them a lien on the crop to be grown. Problems arose because the procedure each had to follow was different.

1. Georgia, *Acts, 1866,* 141.

Strictly construed, the law made it easier for the merchant than for the landlord to get a lien. The merchant's lien came into effect once he made an agreement to provide supplies on credit, and the law did not specify that the agreement be in writing. But the landlord had to make a "special" lien contract in writing before he received a lien on his tenant's crop for any goods he supplied. The distinction almost immediately led to conflict, and the court interpreted the law very strictly to the disadvantage of the landlords. In a case that reached the Georgia Supreme Court in 1868, the evidence showed that a landlord had advanced supplies to a tenant and in return had received a promissory note. The tenant had agreed that the landlord would have a lien on his crop, but the court ruled that because the agreement was not put in writing it did not suffice to create a lien. Unless the promissory note included specific language "showing an intention to create a lien," it did not create a lien under the law. In another case decided that same year, the court ruled that an oral agreement between a farmer and a merchant was sufficient to create a legal lien. The law clearly stated, the court declared, that the landlord's lien had to be in writing but that of "factors and merchants" did not.[2]

The court indicated that it was baffled by the difference between how a landlord and a merchant created a lien for supplies advanced, but it ruled that it had no choice but to construe the law as written: "Why this difference should be made, we confess we do not see. Such, however, is clearly the will of the Legislature as deduced from its words."[3] In any event, the law gave a clear advantage to the merchant. Not only was his lien easier to get—a mere oral agreement gave it the force of law—but also, because to be valid the landlord's lien had to be in writing (and presumably recorded in the local courthouse), the merchant had the added advantage of being able to determine if a potential borrower had already given a lien to his landlord.

Probably the distinction that baffled the court in 1868 did not trouble the lawmakers two years earlier simply because they did not think it would create problems. Their goal was to provide security for advances of supplies to grow a crop, and they could reasonably assume that a renter who received supplies from his landlord would have no reason to look to a merchant for such supplies. But experience soon showed this assumption to be unwar-

2. Wyatt v. Turner, 37 Georgia 640 (1868); Byrd & Crocker v. H. R. Johnson & Co., 38 Georgia 113 (1868).

3. Byrd & Crocker v. H. R. Johnson & Co., 38 Georgia 113 (1868).

ranted. Tenants did borrow from both their landlords and local merchants. Of course, a careful landowner could easily get around the quirk in the law by explicitly creating a lien in writing, but this would not necessarily solve the problem. Far more troublesome was that the law allowed two legal competing liens to exist on the same crop if a tenant borrowed from his landlord, providing the necessary written lien agreement, and from a local merchant.

The law did not rank the two possible liens, probably because the legislators assumed that ranking would be unnecessary, since in most cases only one lien would exist. Only landowners who worked their own land or hired workers or tenants who were not supplied by their landlord would have need to deal with merchants. Moreover, even if there were two legal liens, the lawmakers could assume that existing law — which stipulated that where there were several liens "of the same dignity" on the same property, "then the oldest lien shall have the preference" — would adequately resolve any conflicts.[4]

But the court in the two cases discussed above suggested that the problem of conflicting liens was much more complicated than simply determining the age of each. Existing law, the court explained, seemed to give greater "dignity," that is, priority, to some liens than to others regardless of age. But which liens had that greater dignity was unclear. The court declared that the justices were divided on the question, but in both decisions the court concluded that although lien priority was important, it did not have to rule on the matter because in the particular cases before it the court decided that the landlord did not have a valid lien.[5] As it turned out, multiple liens on the same crop would become increasingly common. Continuing antebellum law, new legislation, and the use of the 1866 lien law in ways that the law's authors did not contemplate regularly created multiple liens where neither the age nor the relative dignity of these multiple liens could be easily determined.

4. *Georgia Code, 1867,* Section 1982, carrying forward antebellum law. The Georgia Code of 1867 was the antebellum code, which the General Assembly ordered prepared in December, 1858, and adopted on December 19, 1860, with postwar revisions. Laws "repealed" or "superseded" were omitted from the 1867 revision, and new laws passed after the war were put in brackets, thereby making it possible to distinguish between antebellum carry-overs and new laws. For a discussion of the history and methods used in preparing the 1867 code, see *Georgia Code, 1867,* iii–xi.

5. Wyatt v. Turner, 37 Georgia 640 (1868); Byrd & Crocker v. H. R. Johnson & Co., 38 Georgia 113 (1868).

Complicating the question of lien priority even further were new conflicts concerning rent, a matter that grew in importance as Georgia landowners, like those elsewhere in the South, increasingly subdivided their lands into small tracts that they rented individually, usually to separate families. These tenants sometimes received needed supplies from their landlord, sometimes from local merchants, but sometimes from both. In such cases, to the possible two liens for supplies was added a third obligation—rent. The landlord's right to his rent arose, of course, from the common law, but Georgia statutes enacted in the early nineteenth century defined and limited common law rights and provided the landowner with a lien for rent. Legislation first passed in 1811, but remaining in the 1867 code, allowed a landlord "to distrain for rent" when it became due or even earlier if the tenant was "seeking to remove his goods from the premises"—that is, the landlord could get a court order to seize the tenant's property and have it sold to insure payment of the rent.[6] Another provision in the same law indicated that the landlord's right to his rent constituted a "lien" on all the tenant's property, including the crop grown.

The law established the priority—or "dignity"—of the landlord's lien for rent in a manner that created problems in the postemancipation era: "The landlord's lien for rent shall attach from the time of levying his distress warrant, but it shall take precedence of no lien of older date except as to the crop raised on the premises." Although this provision clearly stated that the landlord's lien for rent would not reach a tenant's property other than the crop grown if there were an older lien in existence, it did seem to provide that the landlord's lien on the crop for his rent took precedence over other liens on the crop. But the language was far from precise, and as we shall see, the courts did not always grant that precedence. The problem arose from the manner of dating the lien. If the oldest lien on the crop took precedence, then the dating of the landlord's lien for rent became crucial, and if the landlord's lien did not arise until he levied his distress warrant (rather than when he first leased his land) as the law seemed to indicate, then the landlord's lien might not be as old as a merchant's lien for advances. Indeed, a court ruling in 1874 stated that unless the landlord made other

6. "An Act to Point Out the Mode for the Collection of Rents," in Oliver H. Prince (comp.), *Digest of the Laws of the State of Georgia* (Milledgeville, 1822), 394–95. The law was passed on December 16, 1811, and remained unchanged in the *Georgia Code, 1867,* Section 2259–60.

provisions in a specific contract, his lien did not arise until the court levied the distress warrant.[7]

Still another antebellum law that remained in the 1867 code complicated matters even further. This law specifically concerned rental agreements where the rent was a portion of the crop grown, an arrangement that grew increasingly common after the Civil War. It stated that in such cases, none of the tenant's other creditors could press their claims on the portion stipulated as rent. If this law seemed to protect the landlord's rent from other creditors, other provisions in the law significantly limited the landlord's rights. Unlike other rental contracts, which could be oral (so long as they did not exceed a year in duration),[8] contracts for rent to be paid in a portion of the crops produced had to be in writing, and the rent charged could not exceed one-half of the crop.[9]

In sum, then, in December, 1866, after the passage of the first crop lien law in Georgia, a single crop could be encumbered by three separate liens: the landlord's for rent, the landlord's for supplies advanced to his tenant, and a merchant's for supplies advanced to produce a crop. Furthermore, existing law concerning which lien had priority when there were multiple liens was contradictory and ambiguous. Two years later, a new constitution added a fourth possible lien on a single crop—a laborers' lien for wages.

The 1866 lien law and existing antebellum law provided no lien to guarantee that common laborers would be paid,[10] an omission that the lawmakers under Johnson's reconstruction scheme apparently considered unimportant. Black laborers thought otherwise when they were deprived of their wages through fraud and intimidation or when other creditors took the crop or funds their employers had promised to pay them. Although the workers sometimes received support for their claims from sympathetic Freedmen's Bureau officials, state law provided them with no redress other than to sue

7. *Georgia Code, 1867,* Section 2260; Johnson v. Emanuel, 50 Georgia 590 (1874). The latter case considered a dispute that arose prior to 1873 when, as we shall see, the law changed. In its decision the court specifically noted that its ruling was based on the law prior to the Act of 1873.

8. *Georgia Code, 1867,* Section 2254.

9. Georgia, *Acts, 1853–54* (February 14, 1854), 55–56; *Georgia Code, 1867,* Section 2263.

10. Antebellum law still in effect provided liens for skilled workers—mechanics, machinists, steamboat employees, millwrights, and stonecutters—and for providers of services such as lawyers, innkeepers, and common carriers, but made no provisions for common laborers. *Georgia Code, 1867,* Sections 1959, 1966, 1967, 1968, 1973, 1974, 1976, 1979.

as a creditor, an empty right if other creditors with superior legal claims had absorbed their employers' resources. This situation changed after Congress rejected Johnson's reconstruction plan and forced the former Confederate states to write new constitutions embodying its requirements to reenter the Union. Georgia's constitutional convention, elected with blacks voting and including black representatives, provided the laborers with the missing legal protection—a lien on their employers' property. Article I of the 1868 Constitution, a "Declaration of Fundamental Principles," included Section 30: "Mechanics and laborers shall have liens upon the property of their employers for labor performed or material furnished..."

With four different liens possibly encumbering a single crop, the resulting conflicts among landlords, merchants, tenants, and workers over control of the crop are hardly surprising. A few examples of such conflict clearly illustrate how former planters, who had seen the lien laws as a means to support their interests, now sometimes found these laws being used against them in the courts.

In an 1869 case the court deprived a landowner of her rent and gave the proceeds of the crop to a merchant who had provided supplies to the tenants, even though the landlord had a written agreement with the tenants that she would receive half the crop grown as rent, an agreement that predated that of the merchants with the tenants. The court reversed a lower court decision and ruled that when the landlord failed to provide supplies as promised and allowed her tenants to get supplies from a merchant, she in effect waived her lien for rent, although the merchant's lawyers presented no evidence of such a waiver.[11] In another 1869 case, the court ruled in favor of a tenant's claims at the expense of the landlord who had advanced supplies. Two families had agreed to rent land to grow a crop that they would divide evenly between themselves after paying the landowner half as rent. One family in addition contracted in writing with the landlord for supplies.

---

11. Alexander & Howell v. Edmund Glenn *et al.*, 39 Georgia 1 (1869). The issues involved in this case were as follows: In January, 1867, a group of freedmen contracted in writing with a landowner to produce a crop. The landowner "was to furnish them land, seed, quarters, teams, tools and implements, and provisions, and they were to tend the farm, and divide the crop" with the landlord "taking one-half of it." In May of the same year, the freedmen signed a written agreement with the merchants for supplies, reimbursement to come from the crop that would be grown using the supplies. The merchants argued that the landowner had informed them that if they did not provide the necessary supplies, the crop would be lost. They insisted that this meant that the landowner agreed not to press her claims

When the crop was raised, the landlord wanted, in addition to half the crop as his rent, reimbursement from the other half for the advances made, a demand that would have absorbed the remaining crops of both tenants. The tenant who had not contracted for the advances claimed that the landlord's lien for supplies did not reach her portion of the crop even though both tenants had apparently used the supplies advanced. The lower court agreed, and the supreme court upheld the decision, with the result that the landlord was not fully reimbursed for the supplies he had advanced.[12]

In several other decisions, the court dealt with the matter of the priority of various liens, producing decisions that could, and sometimes did, endanger both a landowner's rent and his reimbursement for advances. In a case decided in 1869, the court ruled in favor of a landlord, but its decision suggested potentially grave problems for landlords. The court upheld a lower court decision depriving a merchant of his claim on the grounds that the landlord's claim for rent took precedence. The court, in support of its decision, cited those sections of the antebellum code granting a landlord a lien for his rent,[13] noting that in the instance before it, "the landlord has reduced his lien to writing, and it is older than . . . [the merchant's] lien by a week or two."[14] Obviously implied in this decision was that had the landlord not

---

for half the crop until the merchants' claims were satisfied. The lower court refused to allow the information concerning the landowner's conversation with the merchants to be entered as evidence, and the jury awarded half the proceeds of the crop to the landowner. The supreme court reversed the decision, ruling that the suppressed information was "relevant and material" and gave the merchants the right to the crop they claimed. Although I have used the term *rent* in my summary of the case, it is not entirely clear whether the agreement was between a landlord and tenants or a landlord and workers.

12. McCook v. Cousins, 39 Georgia 125 (1869). Race may have influenced the jury in the lower court and the judges in the appellate court, although there is no direct evidence of such influence. Cousins, the tenant who received her half at the expense of McCook, the landlord, was white. The other tenant, identified in the record only as "Edmund," was black. McCook claimed that although he knew that Cousins and her sons worked on his land along with Edmund and his family, he was unaware of what arrangements the two families had made between themselves and that he had the right to be reimbursed from the proceeds of the entire crop for the supplies he advanced to grow it. Evidence was conflicting on this matter, but the jury accepted the testimony that supported the white tenant, Cousins. The supreme court did not consider the evidence of witnesses; "their credibility was a question for the jury."

13. *Georgia Code, 1867,* Sections 2260 and 2263, discussed above.

14. Toler *et al.* v. Seabrook, 39 Georgia 14 (1869).

put his lien in writing and had his lien not been older than the merchant's, his lien might not have taken precedence, and he would have lost his rent. Indeed, a few years later the Georgia court came to precisely that decision, ruling in 1874, in a case mentioned earlier, that in the absence of a written agreement, the landlord's lien did not arise until the distress warrant was levied, that is, until he convinced the court that his tenant was acting in a manner that might result in the nonpayment of rent.[15] By this time, a merchant might have an earlier lien that would take precedence over the landlord's lien for rent.

In another case decided in 1874, a landlord lost part of his rent and a merchant failed to get reimbursement for advances when the court found existing law that gave a superior lien to another merchant. Events leading to the litigation began in 1872, when George W. Grant leased a cotton farm from Miles G. Dobbins, agreeing to pay as rent five bales of cotton to be produced on the farm. Grant then received fertilizer from a local merchant in return for a lien on the crop. At the end of the season, Grant shipped ten bales of the cotton he had produced to Clark & Cole, a firm described in the evidence as "warehousemen and factors," apparently with orders to sell the cotton. Clark & Cole sold and delivered to the purchaser two of the bales and allowed Grant to take advances on the expected proceeds of the sale of the remaining cotton. To secure these advances, Clark & Cole held the receipts for the stored cotton and entered "indorsements" on them indicating the extent of the advances. In the meantime, the landowner, Dobbins, had not received his rent, and so he asked that Clark & Cole send him the five bales. Clark & Cole sent him the receipts, rather than the cotton, but when the landlord attempted to sell the cotton, he could not do so because of the encumbrances marked on the receipts. Dobbins then asked that Clark & Cole send him the cotton itself, which the latter agreed to do, provided Dobbins paid the advances and any accrued interest. Dobbins refused to pay the advances, and he, joined by the fertilizer merchant, sued to get the cotton free of any encumbrances. When the superior court judge sided with the landlord and the fertilizer merchant, the warehousemen appealed. The supreme court reversed the decision, citing existing law dating from antebellum times that gave factors special rights in goods sent to them, rights that had greater priority than the liens of the landlord and the fertilizer merchant, even though both predated the advances of the factors.[16]

15. Johnson v. Emanuel, 50 Georgia 590 (1874).
16. The lower court ruled that the warehousemen should be paid for any expenses they had incurred but not advances until the landlord and the fertilizer merchant had been paid.

In a case decided the following year, a landlord failed to be repaid for all the advances he had made to a tenant because the court awarded an employee of the tenant part of the crop produced. The case turned not on the rights of workers but rather on the nature of the contract between landlord and tenant. Henry Ware owned a plantation which, "by a verbal contract," he rented to someone identified only by his surname, Harrison. Harrison agreed to "cultivate the place, and furnish the labor," and to pay Ware one-half the crop as rent. In addition, Ware agreed to furnish Harrison with supplies and Harrison agreed to give Ware the remaining half of the crop, which Ware would sell, take payment for the supplies furnished from the proceeds, and then give what remained to Harrison. Harrison then hired Frederick Simmons to work on the land in return for "one-half of all he made."[17] At the end of the year, Harrison gave the worker, Simmons, a bale of cotton, which Ware promptly "took ... from him against his consent" and sold, arguing that the cotton was rightly his because Harrison still owed him money for supplies. Simmons sued, and a jury found the cotton to have been wrongfully taken by Ware and awarded Simmons the value of the cotton. Ware appealed, but the supreme court agreed with the lower court that the verbal contract between a landowner and his tenant for supplies did not create a lien that would take precedence over the payment made to the worker.[18]

An earlier decision also involved the rights of workers. A renter had hired workers and an overseer to direct their work; the overseer was not paid his promised wages, but the court dismissed his suit for payment, ruling that his claim came "before the adoption of the present [1868] Constitu-

---

Clark & Cole v. Miles G. Dobbins *et al.*, 52 Georgia 656 (1874). Antebellum courts had consistently ruled that factors had a lien for advances on the crop after it had been sent to them to be sold. Ordinarily, however, factors had made such advances before receiving the crop, although planters sometimes requested advances on a crop being held by a factor, usually to pay outstanding bills. See pp. 7–8, above. In this instance, there is no evidence that the factors advanced funds before receiving the crop. Nevertheless, the court gave the factors' lien priority over existing liens.

17. Harrison probably hired others as well. The evidence showed that even after making payments for supplies to Ware, Harrison still owed $1,000, which suggests that the operation was a large one. But this case concerned only one worker, Simmons.

18. Ware v. Simmons, 55 Georgia 94 (1875). The reader should recall that this ruling, and those from 1874 that I have discussed, dealt with contracts made before 1873, when, as will be shown, the Georgia legislature enacted new legislation.

tion, providing that laborers shall have a lien.... At common law, and by previous statutes, he had no lien or preference." Presumably also, the laborers who raised the crop had no lien for their wages, but in this instance they received their pay, although not because of the operation of existing state law. The court noted in its summary of the evidence that "the agent of the Freedmen's Bureau took the cotton and corn from the sheriff [after it had been seized by court orders in response to petitions by the landlord and the overseer], and had it sold privately to pay off the wages of the negroes who raised the crop." In its decision the court did not question—or even raise as a relevant issue—the bureau's action, although it meant that the landlord, who received all the produce remaining, did not get his full rent, and the merchant received nothing.[19]

The departure of the Freedmen's Bureau would end its intervention, but existing laws, some dating from antebellum times, some enacted by postbellum conservatives, and some passed by radicals, contained enough ambiguities and contradictions to make the position of the landlords more precarious than they desired. While the radicals were in power, they had little recourse, but once they had overthrown the radical government, Georgia landowners moved quickly to strengthen their position.

In early 1873, the redeemer legislature, in "An Act to regulate the Law of Liens in the State of Georgia,"[20] clarified the lien laws and established lien priorities so as to remove those ambiguities that the landlords had found to be troublesome. The new law gave landlords "a special lien for rent on crops made on lands rented from them, superior to all other liens." The landlord's "special lien for rent" arose automatically without the necessity that it be publicly recorded. Inasmuch as existing antebellum law allowing landlord-tenant contracts up to a year in duration to be oral remained in force, a tenancy and a lien for the rent, superior to all others, could now arise from a simple oral agreement between landlord and tenant, a notation in the planter's records being enough to satisfy the courts that the agreement had been made.[21]

19. Toler *et al.* v. Seabrook, 39 Georgia 14 (1869).
20. Georgia, *Acts, 1873* (February 24, 1873), 42–47.
21. *Georgia Code, 1867,* Section 2254; *Georgia Code, 1882,* Section 2280. The law did not distinguish between rent paid in the form of a portion of a crop and other forms of rent, but it did not specifically repeal the antebellum law (dating from 1853–54) requiring that such rental contracts be limited to one-half the crop and be in writing. The law appears unchanged as Section 2289 in the 1882 *Georgia Code.* Retention of this law seems to have been

The 1873 law also increased the protection of landlords who provided their tenants with supplies. It erased the distinction in the 1866 law between landlord and merchant liens for supplies and gave landlords the means to guarantee that their liens for supplies would take precedence. These provisions, by weakening troublesome competition from merchants, diminished the landlords' risk and significantly increased their ability to control the working as well as the private lives of their tenants.

The law granted liens on crops to "factors, merchants, landlords, dealers in fertilizers, and all other persons furnishing supplies, money, farming utensils, or other articles of necessity to make crops, and also all persons furnishing clothing and medicines, supplies or provisions for the support of families, or medical services, tuition or school books." It stipulated that all such liens "must be created by special contract, in writing," and further, that anyone giving a lien for such items had to inform the person making the advances of any other liens already given, the amount of such liens, and the person to whom given. These provisions increased the number of potential lenders who could get a lien on a crop; the 1866 law listed only factors, merchants, and landlords. They also extended the range of items that could be covered by a lien; the 1866 law listed specific items—stock, farm equipment, provisions, and fertilizer—advanced to tenants "for the purpose of making their crops," provisions that the courts had construed very strictly, thereby destroying what seemed to be legitimate liens.[22] Finally, by requiring all suppliers to put their agreements in writing, the new law ended the advantage enjoyed by merchants under the old law.

Now *all* liens for supplies had to be in writing. But the ostensible equal-

---

an oversight on the part of the legislature. I have found no cases in which the litigants used the law in their arguments and have discovered no evidence that it was formally repealed, but it no longer appears in the 1895 *Code*.

22. In 1873 the supreme court affirmed lower court decisions that dismissed a merchant's claim for liens on planters' crops because the advances were in the form of money rather than supplies. The law explicitly said that merchants and factors had a lien for supplies advanced, and it did not matter, the court ruled, that the money was advanced with the stated intention that it was to be used to buy supplies and was in fact used to buy supplies. Had the legislature in 1866 intended to include "money advanced to purchase provision . . . it would have said so." Therefore, one who advanced money did not qualify for a lien. Saulsbury, Repess & Company v. S. E. Eason, 47 Georgia 617 (1873). Two other cases under appeal by Saulsbury, Repess & Company were also involved in this decision. See also Speer v. Hart, 45 Georgia 113 (1872).

ity in requirements for all lenders, in fact, gave the landlords an advantage. Because the antebellum law granting the earliest lien priority over subsequent liens remained, a landlord could guarantee the priority of his lien for supplies by making his lien contract for supplies to be furnished at the time he rented his land. Because the law declared that liens from a previous year's crop did not carry over to the new crop, the landlord could be reasonably confident that merchants or other lenders would not have provided an advance and taken a lien on a new crop to be grown before a landless farmer had rented land on which to grow the crop. In any event, he could simply ask a potential tenant if he had already given a lien and refuse to lease land to anyone who had already encumbered the future crop.

Including cash and personal items among the goods advanced that could create a lien gave landlords the power to exercise considerable control over their tenants' work and their private lives as well. By granting or withholding such items, the landlord could affect the day-to-day living conditions of his tenants; he could be confident that if he periodically withheld such items to punish a recalcitrant tenant, the tenant would be unable to secure them elsewhere because the landlord's earlier lien would take precedence.[23] Another provision in the new law increased even further the landlords' ability to control their tenants' work and well-being. In addition to his special crop lien for rent, the landlord could also get a "general lien on the property of the debtor" for his rent, thus allowing him to reach all of his tenant's property, not just the crop he grew, should that crop not be sufficient to pay the rent. This general lien was also automatic—the law did not stipulate that it had to be in writing—and it ranked with other liens "according to date." But by putting this general lien in writing at the time he made his rental agreement, the landlord could guarantee its priority, thereby closing off the tenant's opportunity to mortgage his property as a means to get advances from someone other than his landlord. Should such a tenant end the year without having produced enough to pay his rent, his landlord could seize his property—mules, equipment, and personal items—to satisfy the debt.[24]

23. The lien was for all supplies advanced over the crop year even if the goods were advanced piecemeal during the year.

24. Of course, a tenant who agreed to pay a portion of what he grew as rent was unaffected by this provision in the law. But those who rented for cash (to be paid from the proceeds of the crop grown) and those with what was called a "standing rent" agreement (a given number of bales or bushels at the end of the year) would be affected. Inasmuch as the cash and standing renters were more likely to own valuable property than were share renters,

Although the 1873 law enormously strengthened the landlord's position at the expense of his tenants and the merchants, the potential for conflict remained. The landlord's rent was secure, but merchants and others could still get a lien on the crops of tenants for advances, and if the landlord failed to request and record his lien or took his lien without asking whether his tenant had already given a lien to someone else,[25] he could find himself without adequate security for any advances he made. A year later, the Georgia legislature obligingly provided landlords with complete monopoly protection by closing the remaining door open to merchants and others who advanced supplies. It repealed that section of the law that allowed "factors, merchants, dealers in fertilizers, and other persons" to receive liens on crops on which they had made advances, reserving such liens solely to advances by landlords.[26]

The legislature quickly realized, however, that it had closed the door too tightly. If tenants could not borrow and give a lien to anyone other than the landowner from whom they rented, then the landlords might be forced to supply their tenants even when they preferred not to. Landlords without adequate resources of their own would have to borrow from merchants in order to supply their tenants, but such borrowing by landlords, as well as by small farmers, would be more difficult because the lending merchants would no longer be able to get a lien to secure their loans. Before the 1874 legislation could have such unwanted results, the legislature changed the law once again.[27]

New legislation in 1875 solved this problem and did so in a way that provided additional protection for the landlord. All who provided supplies could get a lien on the crop, but when landlords supplied their tenants, their

---

this provision was an important safeguard for the landlord. Furthermore, landlords who desired to do so might insist that tenancies be for cash or standing rent, especially in cases where a tenant owned mules, farm equipment, or other property of value.

25. The law exacted criminal penalties when a borrower, "if interrogated," did not inform a lender of previous liens, but it did not require that the tenant volunteer that information.

26. Georgia, *Acts, 1874* (February 2, 1874), 18.

27. The 1874 law, although approved on February 20, was not to go into effect until November, that is, after the close of the crop year. The new law discussed below was approved on February 25, 1875, the start of the new crop year. Thus, the legislature recognized the problems the 1874 law would have created and changed the law before the start of a new crop year.

liens "shall arise by operation of law from the relation of landlord and tenant." This meant that the landlord automatically received a lien on his tenant's crop for any advances he might provide without the need to put the agreement in writing. But the landlord could, should he so desire, also get his lien through a "special contract in writing." Another provision indicated why he might choose to do so: "whenever said liens may be created by special contract in writing . . . the same shall be assignable by the landlord."[28] Thus, those planters who wanted to maximize their control over tenants and minimize the risk from competing liens were assured superior liens on their tenants' crops for both rent and advances. A simple oral agreement to rent land automatically gave the landlord a superior lien on his tenant's crop for rent and for any supplies he provided during the year. Those landlords who preferred to avoid the expense, trouble, and risk could allow merchants to supply their tenants without losing their liens for rent simply by putting a supply agreement in writing and then assigning it to someone else. The decision to retain or assign a lien for supplies and other items rested entirely with the landlord, and if he decided to assign his lien, he and not the tenant or the merchant chose the person to whom he assigned the rights.

If by 1875 the Georgia legislature had provided landlords with dominance over both their tenants and local merchants, the laws did not force the merchants out of the trade with planters and their tenants, nor did they end all conflicts. Landlords had to be aware of their rights under the law and take the steps necessary to protect those rights. For example, in a case decided in 1888, the court ruled that a landlord could lose his lien for rent if he failed to protect it from innocent buyers. A tenant had sold the crop in his possession without first paying his rent. When the landlord sued the buyer for recovery on the grounds that he had a superior lien for rent, the court ruled that in this instance the purchase was legitimate, and therefore the buyer was protected: "Landlords generally are on or near the rented premises, and have better opportunities to look after their rights and interests than purchasers would ordinarily have." Of course, the renter remained indebted, and the landlord could bring a civil or a criminal suit against him, since it was a misdemeanor to sell a crop on which there was a lien for rent. If convicted, the tenant could be assessed double damages, half going to the landlord with the lien,[29] but winning a civil suit against a propertyless tenant

28. Georgia, *Acts, 1875* (February 25, 1875), 20.
29. Thornton v. Carver, 80 Georgia 397, 6 S.E. 915 (1888). Apparently the legal prin-

could be a pyrrhic victory, and the courts made criminal suits difficult to sustain.[30]

Many merchants remained in business because some landlords preferred to deal with them either directly by borrowing from them and then advancing supplies to their tenants or indirectly by agreeing to allow particular merchants to supply their tenants. In the former arrangement, the merchant had a lien on the planter's crop and the planter in turn would get a lien on the tenant's crop for both rent and advances. In the latter arrangement, the planter kept his lien for rent, but the merchant received a lien on the tenant's crop for advances. In practice, variations on these arrangements and ambiguities in oral and written contracts led to continuing disagreements among merchants, tenants, and landlords, disagreements that sometimes led to litigation. The issues involved in these cases reveal the variations in tenancy and credit arrangements and the continuing role of merchants in these arrangements despite the dominant legal position of the landowners.

Should a landlord prefer not to supply his tenants and allow a merchant to do so, the law allowed the merchant to get a lien on the tenants' crops

---

ciple the court applied in this case was that which protected a bona fide or innocent purchaser, that is, one who makes a purchase without knowledge or the reasonably accessible means to acquire knowledge that the title to the property is encumbered. Given the nature of the lien laws, few local buyers could claim the status of innocent buyer, although buyers at a distance occasionally did so. In Mississippi, for example, the court ruled that the state's lien laws "have no extraterritorial effect," that when agricultural products were sent to merchants in another state "the lien ceased to follow." In the absence of a conspiracy between the tenant and the merchants to cheat the landlord, the merchants could be considered innocent buyers. Although the merchants knew of the existence of Mississippi's law creating a lien for rent, "they had reason to think ... that the landlord would look after his own rights, and not permit the shipment of cotton until his rent demand had been satisfied." Millsaps v. Tate, 75 Mississippi 150, 21 So. 663 (1897). See also Sternberger v. McSween, 14 South Carolina 35 (1880).

30. To sustain a criminal conviction against a tenant who sold any part of a crop before paying rent and advances due under his landlord's lien, the state had to prove that the landlord did not give his consent to the sale, that the sale was made with intent to defraud the landlord, and that the landlord suffered a loss because of the sale. Despite these limitations, tenants were sometimes convicted. See Morrison v. State, 111 Georgia 642, 36 S.E. 902 (1900); Kellam v. State, 2 Georgia App. 479, 58 S.E. 695 (1907); Reece v. State, 5 Georgia App. 663, 63 S.E. 690 (1909); McGarr v. State, 13 Georgia App. 80, 78 S.E. 776 (1913); Smith v. State, 17 Georgia App. 554, 87 S.E. 829 (1916); Sims v. State, 43 Georgia App. 438, 158 S.E. 913 (1931).

for the supplies advanced. No problem would arise so long as the landlord provided no supplies and allowed his tenants to make their own arrangements. Often, however, matters became more complicated. A landlord who preferred not to supply his tenants himself might want them to deal with a merchant of his choosing, an arrangement, it will be recalled, the law allowed, provided the landlord and his tenant entered into a written contract that the landlord then assigned to the merchant; this gave the merchant the landlord's superior lien for supplies advanced. The court insisted that landlords adhere to the letter of this law, refusing to accept assignments in the absence of a written contract and ruling also that the written contract and the assignment of the lien had to be executed before the tenant made any arrangements for credit on his own. If the tenant had already given a lien for advances to a merchant, then that merchant had a superior lien, even if the landlord and the tenant later agreed to a contract that the landlord assigned to another merchant.[31]

The creation of other forms of debt instruments added to the legal complications concerning liens, complications that could endanger the protection the law granted landlords. Under some circumstances, a landlord could become liable for his tenant's debts without having the protection of a lien on the tenant's crop. For example, if a landlord asked a merchant to supply his tenant, the merchant often demanded that the agreement with the tenant be endorsed by the landlord. Although this endorsement meant that the landlord agreed to pay his tenant's bill should the tenant fail to do so, the Georgia Supreme Court ruled that simply providing security for a tenant's advances did not automatically give the landlord a lien for advances.[32] Even when a landlord paid his tenant's bill for supplies, this did not necessarily give him a lien on the tenant's crop for advances. Evidence in a case decided in 1889 indicated that a landlord received from a dealer fertilizer that he then provided to his tenant, taking in return a note payable to the fertilizer dealer. Although the landlord rather than the tenant ultimately paid the note, the court ruled that this arrangement did not give the landlord a lien for supplies on the tenant's crop; the landlord had simply acted as an "agent" for the merchant.[33] Under such circumstances, others could have a legiti-

31. Elliott v. Parker, 94 Georgia 620, 20 S. E . 106 (1894).
32. Scott v. Pound, 61 Georgia 579 (1878); Brimberry v. Mansfield, 86 Georgia 792, 13 S.E. 132 (1891).
33. Swann v. Morris, 83 Georgia 143, 9 S.E. 767 (1889).

mate lien that could absorb the tenant's crop, leaving the landlord without compensation.

The landlord therefore had to exercise care in order to retain his lien protection when making arrangements with a merchant to supply his tenants. If the landlord was the agent for the merchant, the landlord did not have a lien, but, the court ruled, if the merchant was merely the agent of the landlord—that is, if he supplied the landlord's tenants, but the agreement between landlord and merchant with the tenants' consent was that the landlord be billed for the supplies—then the landlord had a lien for supplies even though he did not deliver the supplies directly to the tenants. Similarly, if the landlord provided his tenant with money to buy the supplies, the court considered this the same as the landlord providing supplies himself and ruled that the landlord had the lien.[34]

Because so many agreements were small-scale and made without legal advice, interpretation of their meaning could be controversial, as a decision in 1896 revealed. The evidence showed that a tenant had provided a merchant with a promissory note for supplies advanced that the landlord had endorsed; the landlord claimed that his endorsement, which made him responsible for the tenant's debt, entitled him to a lien for advances. The law in this case was clear, according to the court, but the facts were not. "A landlord is not entitled to a lien upon his tenant's crop for supplies, unless the same are furnished by the landlord himself," the court declared, but added that if the landlord's endorsement was made with the tenant's consent and "in fact" made the landlord "the real purchaser," he would have the lien just as if he had provided the advances himself. Determining who was the "real purchaser" was a question of "fact," not law, and therefore "the truth of the matter ... [was] a question for the jury."[35]

Leaving the question of "fact" to the jury resolved particular cases but hardly ended controversy because the evidence when conflict led to litigation was usually contradictory. In a dispute that came before an appeals court in 1908, the court admitted that the evidence presented to the jury in the lower court that led it to decide in favor of the landlord might reasonably have led it to decide in favor of a merchant, but it concluded that there was enough evidence to "have authorized the jury's verdict, and we have no

34. Boyce v. Day, 3 Georgia App. 275, 95 S. E . 930 (1907); Phillips v. Freeman, 30 Georgia App. 450, 118 S.E. 104 (1923); Fargason v. Ford, 119 Georgia 343, 46 S.E. 431 (1904).
35. Rodgers v. Black, 99 Georgia 139, 25 S.E. 23 (1896).

power to set aside a verdict which is authorized by the evidence, where no error of law has been committed."[36]

This case illustrated how important the jury's decision could be in sorting out the complicated arrangements among landlords, tenants, and merchants when a crop produced could not satisfy all creditors. The controversy arose when a merchant who had advanced supplies to the tenant claimed that his lien took precedence over the landlord's claims. The landlord had allowed his tenant to get advances from a store on his plantation, and the merchant argued that because the landlord and his tenant had no written agreement for advances that the landlord assigned to the merchant who ran the plantation store, the landlord did not have a superior lien for advances. However, the jury decided that the merchant on the plantation was merely the agent of the landlord. Therefore, the court ruled, the landlord was really providing the advances, making a written agreement and an assignment unnecessary. Had the jury found that the merchant running the plantation store was independent and not the agent of the landlord, then the absence of a written and assigned agreement would have meant that the landlord did not have a prior lien and the complaining merchant would have had first call on the crop for his advances.

In sum, then, the laws as enacted by the redeemer legislatures in Georgia and as interpreted by the courts clearly favored the landlords, offering them ample protection for their rents and for any advances they made to their tenants. If landlords chose to do so, they could exclude merchants from dealing with their tenants—or, more precisely, they could make any liens given to merchants by their tenants inferior to their liens. At the same time, however, landlords could elect to allow their tenants to make their own arrangements with merchants of their choosing or they could assign their liens to merchants they, rather than their tenants, selected. Because many landlords preferred to turn the supply business over to merchants and because many landlords themselves borrowed from merchants, ample business opportunities remained for merchants, and the lien laws in such instances protected them.

The pattern of legal change in Mississippi, South Carolina, and North Carolina was similar to that in Georgia. Landowners in these states who leased lands and provided their tenants with supplies to grow a crop also

36. Henderson v. Hughes, 4 Georgia App. 52, 60 S.E. 813 (1908).

faced the unanticipated threat that they would not receive their rent and repayment for supplies advanced. Although in the Carolinas the Republican legislatures proved somewhat more accommodating to the landowners than were the radicals in Georgia and Mississippi, not until redemption did the landowners in these states have the power to rank debts in a manner that fully protected them.

Mississippi's 1867 crop lien law granted a lien to anyone advancing supplies to grow a crop, but because neither this legislation nor existing law provided the landlord with a lien for rent,[37] the court ruled that the landlord's right to his rent was subordinate to a lien the tenant provided to a merchant for supplies.[38] The 1867 law required that the lien for advances "shall be filed" with the local county clerk, and the court decided that unless or until it were so recorded, it did not constitute a lien under the law.[39] Therefore, if a merchant delayed recording his lien, it would lose its precedence over other claims.[40] But the purpose of the requirement that liens be recorded, the court explained, was to protect potential merchant lenders, not landlords. Those approached for an advance could easily discover the existence and extent of any earlier liens before providing credit by examining the lien record books in the local courthouse.[41]

Thus a Mississippi landowner who leased his lands might lose his rents to merchants who supplied his tenants. Of course, the landlord had a legal right to his rent, and he could sue a delinquent tenant for nonpayment, but because the supplier had a lien he could legally absorb the tenant's entire crop, leaving nothing to pay the rent. A landlord could write a contract with the express stipulation that it created a lien on the crop to be produced for rent and advances, and this lien would be valid, the court ruled, but only so long as it did not interfere with the rights of third parties. Unfortunately, from the landlord's perspective, those third parties could be nu-

37. Mississippi, *Acts, 1866–67* (February 18, 1867), 569–72; Stewart v. Hollins *et al.,* 47 Mississippi 708 (1873); Doctor Doty v. John T. Heth, 52 Mississippi 530 (1876).

38. Stamps v. Gillman, 43 Mississippi 456 (1870).

39. Bain v. Brooks, 46 Mississippi 537 (1872).

40. In a case decided in 1870, the court ruled that although the 1867 law made the lien for advances superior to any later judgment against the crop grown, if the advancer delayed recording his lien, a judgment entered before the lien was recorded would be superior to the lien even if the supplies advanced had been used to grow the crop on which the judgment had been executed. Howard v. Simmons, 43 Mississippi 75 (1870).

41. French v. Picard, 49 Mississippi 320 (1873).

merous. They might be merchants who agreed to supply advances and recorded their agreements before those of the landlords, and after the new government elected under radical reconstruction came to power, they could also be workers who, by legislation in 1872 and 1873, were given a superior lien for their wages. As a result, the possibility of a variety of liens on a single crop, many that could be superior to the landlord's claim for rent, created considerable uncertainty among landowners who leased their property.[42]

The radicals apparently felt no need to change the law in order to give the landlords greater protection, and therefore the position of the landlord in Mississippi remained precarious until the fall of the radicals in November, 1875. The new redeemer legislature promptly provided the landlords with the missing protection they sought. A new law granted a "lien in favor of landlords" for both rent and advances. The landlord's rental contract did not have to be in writing, and his liens did not have to be officially recorded to be valid. The landlord's lien for rent was superior to all other liens; his lien for supplies was subordinate to that of another supplier's advance only when it preceded that of the landlord and even then, only if the landlord had received "notice" of the earlier advance.[43]

Less than a year later the legislature clarified its intention to insure the dominance of landlords' liens. A new law stipulated that the term "notice"

---

42. White v. Thomas, 52 Mississippi 49 (1876), a case involving an agreement made in 1871; Mississippi, *Laws* (April 5, 1872), 134; Mississippi, *Laws* (April 17, 1873), 79–81. The laborers' lien laws will be discussed in the following chapter. In several decisions, the court broadly construed the laws granting a superior lien to workers for their wages to rule that they gave the landlords a lien for rent. The first section of the 1873 laborers' lien law indicated that the laborers' lien "shall extend to and apply as well to the interest or share of the crop of the landlord for the rent of the land on which such crop may be raised," a provision designed to protect workers hired by renters as well as owners of land. In decisions involving disputes between landlords and tenants (workers were not involved), the court ruled that these words indicated that the landlord had a lien. See Arbuckle v. Nelms, 50 Mississippi 556 (1874), and Storm v. Green, 51 Mississippi 103 (1875). But the extent of that lien remained uncertain. In Phillips v. Douglass, 53 Mississippi 175 (1876), the court ruled that the landlord had the lien only if rent was for a share of the crop but not for money rentals. And in a later decision, made after the redeemers changed the law, the court in effect dismissed this construction of the laborers' lien laws, ruling that there was "no lien for rent in this state until the recent statutes establishing it." Doctor Doty v. John T. Heth, 52 Mississippi 530 (1876).

43. Mississippi, *Acts, 1876* (April 14, 1876), 109–110.

in the 1876 law should be construed as "actual" rather than "constructive"—that is, merely putting the other lien in writing and recording it in the courthouse where the landlord could see it would not suffice; the landlord had to be told of any earlier liens before they could become superior to his. Even this minor reservation soon disappeared. By 1880, suppliers were limited to mortgages on growing crops, and these mortgages were always inferior to the landlord's lien for both rent and advances.[44]

If the redeemers in Mississippi, like those in Georgia, completely subordinated all claims to a crop to the liens of the landlord for rent and advances, they did not completely end business opportunities for merchants. A landlord who so desired could assign his lien to someone else or waive all or part of his lien, but, as in Georgia, the decision was his and not the tenant's to make.[45] A Mississippi landlord could simply refrain from supplying his tenants and let them get advances on their own, and if a merchant under these circumstances demanded that the landlord endorse or guarantee payment of such advances, the Mississippi court, like the Georgia court, ruled that if a landlord merely guaranteed payment for supplies furnished by a merchant, the landlord did not have a lien for supplies.[46] Finally, should a merchant contract to supply a tenant and inform the landlord of his arrangement, the landlord could not decide at a later date to furnish the supplies and get a superior lien on the crop, unless the merchant did not in fact provide the supplies.[47]

South Carolina's first lien law in 1866 did not mention rents. It gave "any person or persons" advancing supplies to make a crop a lien on the crop "in preference of all other liens existing or otherwise," provided the agreement was in writing. If the landlord was the "person" advancing supplies he could have a superior lien for such advances. The landlord could enter into a rental contract with his tenants that gave him a lien for rent, but this lien would be inferior to any lien for supplies, even if the landlord's rental contract was written and recorded, stated that it created a lien, and predated that of the supplier's lien. Uncontested evidence in a case that reached the

44. Mississippi, *Acts, 1877* (January 27, 1877), 83; Mississippi, *Code, 1880,* Chapter 51, Section 1301. See Newman *et al.* v. Bank of Greenville *et al.*, 66 Mississippi 323, 5 So. 753 (1889) for the Mississippi Supreme Court's summary of the legislative history of the laws.

45. Taylor v. Nelson, 54 Mississippi 524 (1877); Dreyfus *et al.* v. W. A. Gage & Co., 84 Mississippi 219, 36 South 248 (1904).

46. Ellis v. Jones, 70 Mississippi 60, 11 So. 566 (1892).

47. Paxton v. Meyer, 58 Mississippi 445 (1880).

South Carolina Supreme Court in 1873 indicated that a renter had given a landlord a lien for rent on the crops to be grown and that the lien had been written and recorded on February 20, 1871. A month later (March 20) the renter gave a lien to a merchant for supplies, which the merchant recorded on April 6. When the crop produced could not pay both debts, the court ruled that the 1866 law gave the supplier's lien priority over the lien for rent even though it was of a later date. "The Act gives no lien for the use of the land—but only for what is necessary for the cultivation of the land itself," the court explained. In another case decided the same year, the court justified its decision to give priority to the suppliers' liens by clearly and accurately revealing the underlying assumption of the conservative legislators who wrote the original lien law: landowners expected to hire former slaves to work their lands, and they needed the lien law to secure the credit needed to pay such hired labor. "Its design was to promote the agricultural interests of the State by encouraging the cultivation of lands, which would otherwise be unproductive for the want of supplies to support the labor which could be readily furnished."[48]

The lack of protection for the landlord's rent became increasingly serious when growing numbers of planters began to rent small parcels to their former slaves. The radical legislature acted to provide a measure of protection for the landlords but did so in a manner that denied them a monopoly and gave tenants considerable protection, suggesting that its primary purpose was to encourage small-scale tenancy, which the freedmen preferred, rather than to protect the landlords. A law approved on March 19, 1874, made rent a form of supplies and provided that when land was rented, the rent would be "deemed and taken to be an advance for agricultural purposes" which gave the landlord "all the rights accorded to persons advancing money and other supplies" under the 1866 law. The new law limited such liens for rent to no more than one-third of the crop and required that they be recorded.[49]

By making rent a form of the supplies covered by the 1866 lien law, the legislature made it possible for a landlord to get a lien for rent and a merchant to get a lien for supplies. Because both liens, in the language of the 1866 legislation, were "in preference to all others," the new law created the po-

48. South Carolina, *Acts, 1866* (September 20, 1866), 380–81; Dunn v. Spears, 5 South Carolina 17 (1873); Visanska v. Bradley, 4 South Carolina 288 (1873).
49. South Carolina, *Acts, 1873–74,* 788–89.

tential for landlord-merchant conflict when the landlord was not the tenant's sole supplier and the crop produced could not satisfy both a merchant's and a landlord's claims. Limiting the rent covered by the lien to one-third of the crop put a ceiling on rents—or, at least, on rents protected by a superior lien—and gave the tenant, with two-thirds of a crop on which to offer a lien, the opportunity to encourage landlord-merchant competition for his business. Tenants undoubtedly welcomed both the protection and the competition the law provided, but the landlords did not.

When the redeemers finally took control in 1877, they responded to landlord frustration with existing law by repealing all the lien laws, a draconian measure that, had it actually gone into force, would have simply created new problems to replace the old. Without the lien laws, landlords had diminished security for their rents, and all lenders were without security for their loans. Before the repeal could have such negative results, the legislature reenacted the lien laws in "An Act to Secure Landlords and Persons Making Advances." This time, however, the landlords received special protection. The new law made the landlord's lien for rent "prior and preferred" to all other liens. The lien for rent for up to one-third of the crop did not have to be written and recorded, but the landlord could get a superior lien for higher rents by recording the amount in excess of one-third. A supplier's lien had to be in writing and was inferior to that of the landlord for rent, but it was superior to all others.[50]

The legislature had decided to proceed cautiously, stipulating that the new law, enacted in March, 1878, would remain in force for only one year, but by December the lawmakers were apparently satisfied with the results of the new legislation and passed an amendment extending the law "in full force without limitation." The legislators immediately realized that they had not gone far enough to please the landlords, who now had superior protection for their rent but not for any advances they might make to tenants. Three days after extending the earlier law, the legislature passed another, whose purpose was openly declared in its title to be "for the further protection of landlords in the collection of moneys due by tenants for rents and advances." The new law extended the landlord's superior lien for rent to include his advances as well. In addition, it provided that the landlord's liens

50. South Carolina, *Acts, 1877* (June 8, 1877), 265 (although approved on June 8, 1877, the lien law repeal was not to take effect until January 1, 1878); South Carolina, *Acts, 1877–78* (March 4, 1878), 410–11.

"shall extend to all crops raised on the lands leased by the landlords, whether the same be raised by the tenant or other persons," a provision that allowed the landlord's lien to extend through his tenant to encumber the crops of any sub-tenants or workers the tenant hired.[51]

Additional legislation during the 1880s added to the landlords' protection. New legislation removed the stipulation that liens for rent in excess of one-third of the crop be in writing and explicitly provided that the liens were valid for both written and oral rental contracts and "took effect from the date of the contract." Both landlords and others could still get liens for advances to tenants, but while legislation explicitly required that merchants' advances be written and recorded, it was less clear concerning landlords' liens for supplies. After nearly two decades of confusing and contradictory decisions on this matter, the court, in a sharply divided and close decision, finally ruled in 1914 that the landlord's lien for advances did not have to be recorded, thereby insuring landlord dominance over both merchants and tenants.[52]

North Carolina's first lien law in 1867 provided a superior lien to "any person or persons" making an advance but included a provision that stated that the lien for advances did not affect the landlord's right to his "proper share" for rent. As we have seen, the landlord's right to his rent did not constitute a lien on the crop but rather, as defined by a law enacted at the same time, a kind of quasi-ownership of that portion of the crop due for rent, an arrangement that preserved traditional landlord-tenant relations in the state but created enough ambiguity to cause considerable uncertainty.[53]

In 1869, the legislature repealed this ambiguous definition of the landlord's right to his rent when it rewrote the landlord-tenant law. Although North Carolina Republicans still controlled the legislature in 1869 (control they would overwhelmingly lose the following year), they showed far more concern for the landlords than did Republicans elsewhere in the South. The new law removed the ambiguous definition of the landlord's right to his rent

51. South Carolina, *Acts, 1878* (December 20, 1878), 713–14; South Carolina, *Acts, 1878* (December 23, 1878), 743–44.

52. South Carolina, *Civil Code, 1902,* Sections 3057 and 3059; Nexsen v. Ward *et al.*, 96 South Carolina 313, 80 S.E. 599 (1914). This decision contains a good summary of legislation and the various decisions.

53. North Carolina, *Public Laws, 1866–67* (March 1, 1867), 3–4. See the discussion of the North Carolina legislation giving landlords a quasi-ownership of tenants' crops for rents due in Chapter 1, pp. 12–14.

and provided him with protection in a manner that undermined traditional landlord-tenant relations:

> It shall be competent for any lessee of land to agree in writing to pay the lessor a share of the crop to be grown on the land during the term as rent, or to give him a lien on the whole crop, or any part thereof, as a security for the performance of any stipulation contained in the lease; and when the lessee has so agreed, such charge, or such crop, shall be deemed to be held to be vested in possession in the lessor and his assigns at all times until such lien shall have been satisfied or discharged.

Although the new law did not automatically grant the landlord a lien, it allowed him to receive a lien by entering into a written contract with his tenant that gave him a lien, which in turn gave the landlord legal possession of the crop until the tenant paid the rent. In short, under the new law the landlord was not merely a preferred creditor of the tenant, as traditional law would have it, but the owner of the tenant's crop until he took his rent. Therefore, it followed that a tenant who removed any part of the crop he was producing before meeting rent obligations was guilty of theft, a criminal act rather than simply an abridgment of contract. The law made this explicit, declaring that a tenant who had given his landlord a lien for rent, or anyone else who had knowledge of the lien, who removed any part of the crop without the consent of the landlord "shall be guilty of a misdemeanor."[54]

Although the new law clearly and unambiguously secured the landlord's rent, it was not explicit about any supplies the landlord might have advanced to his tenants. Inasmuch as the original crop lien law allowing a supplier to get a lien on a crop remained unchanged, the status of the landlord's lien for supplies relative to that of a merchant's remained uncertain. Presumably, the written rental agreement could include payment for any supplies the landlord provided, which would give the landlord complete protection from any merchant claims until the landlord received full compensation for rent and advances.

54. North Carolina, *Public Laws, 1868–69* (April 10, 1869), 355–74. Although the sections of the law quoted dealt with rent to be paid in the form of a share of the crop, another section of the new law stipulated that the same provisions and penalties covered money rentals.

If, however, the landlord failed to secure a written contract explicitly spelling out his rights to rent and advances, then he did not have these rights. In a case decided in 1874, the North Carolina Supreme Court ruled that a landlord who rented for a share of the crop and did not put the agreement in writing "cannot claim a lien" under the law of 1869 either for rent or for the advances he had provided to grow the crop. Therefore, a merchant with whom the tenant had made an agreement for supplies could legally take the crop that the landlord had claimed was his for rent and advances: "By permitting his right both to rent and to compensation for his advances to rest on the oral promise of Moss [the tenant] and without any agreement for a lien, he [the landlord] lost all other remedy than by an action on such oral promise."[55]

Once in power, the redeemers amended the landlord and tenant act to remove this potential threat to the landlord. The new law provided that when a landlord, by either "written or verbal" contract, rented his land and provided advances to his tenants, "any and all crops raised on said land shall be deemed and held to be vested in the possession in the owner of the land" until liens and advances were paid, and further, that the landlord's rights to rent and advances constituted a lien that "shall be preferred to all other liens."[56] Merchants could still get liens for advances, but the merchants' liens would be subordinate to those of the landowners, unless, as allowed by the new law, the landlord chose to assign his superior liens to others.

The effect of this law was to give the landlords overwhelming statutory power over their tenants—more, in fact, than they enjoyed in other states. By giving the landlord "possession" rather than simply lien rights in the crop, the law completely destroyed traditional landlord-tenant relations.[57] Indeed, so complete was the landlord's control over his tenant's crop under the 1875 law that the legislature amended it two years later to prevent abuse. The landlord's possession and lien rights remained unchanged, but a new provision allowed the tenant or his "assigns" to demand that the landlord "make a fair division" of the crop once the tenant had met his obligations. This pre-

55. Harrison v. Ricks, 71 North Carolina 7 (1874).
56. North Carolina, *Laws, 1874–75* (March 19, 1875), 281–83.
57. The court ruled that the crop was in possession of the landlord until his liens were satisfied. Durham v. Speeke, 82 North Carolina 87 (1880). As I shall indicate in the next chapter, this right of possession enjoyed by landlords was a key feature of cropping, not tenancy. The effect of the 1875 North Carolina law was to make all tenants into croppers.

vented the landlord who had possession of the entire crop from unfairly delaying division, thereby retaining possession of the tenant's legitimate share, including that part that he may have promised to others.[58]

Antebellum law in Louisiana, like that in the Carolinas, protected the landlord's right to his rent, but the evolution of the laws in Louisiana differed somewhat from that elsewhere, largely because of the continuing influence of New Orleans merchants. The Louisiana legislature organized under Johnsonian reconstruction allowed the antebellum law granting a "privilege" (that is, a lien) to landlords for rent to remain unchanged, but in 1867, in its version of the crop lien law, it specifically listed a number of other "privileged" debts, including those owed to parties who provided supplies or money to buy supplies necessary to produce a crop. The privileges, the law stated, "shall be concurrent," that is, having the same authority. Inasmuch as the law did not mention rents and the article in the antebellum code granting a privilege to the landlord for rent remained, the ranking of the various "concurrent" privileged debts was uncertain.[59]

But such uncertainties did not concern the conservative legislators. Most of the provisions in the new law merely carried forward the antebellum law concerning factor-planter relations and reflected the assumption of the legislators that large-scale production on the antebellum pattern would continue with wage labor replacing slave labor and that New Orleans would continue to be the key commercial center for the sale of the staple crops, the city's merchants receiving consignments not only from Louisiana but from the entire Mississippi Valley as they had before the war. Merchant in-

---

58. North Carolina, *Laws, 1876–77* (March 12, 1877), 551.

59. The Louisiana Code defined a privilege as "a right, which the nature of a debt gives to a creditor, and which entitles him to be preferred before other creditors, even those who have a mortgage" (*Civil Code of Louisiana, 1825,* Article 3153; *Revised Civil Code of the State of Louisiana, 1870,* Section 3186). This made the privilege, under Louisiana Roman Law, the same as a lien elsewhere. The legislation used the word *privilege,* as did the courts, although occasionally court decisions used the word *lien* when referring to a privilege. See *Civil Code of Louisiana, 1825,* Article 3185; *Revised Civil Code of the State of Louisiana, 1870,* Section 3218; Louisiana, *Acts, 1867* (March 28, 1867), 351–53 (which "amended and re-enacted" Article 3184 of the *Civil Code of Louisiana, 1825*). In addition to adding the privilege granted to suppliers, the latter law made the wages of workers a privileged debt on the crop and dropped reference to a debt owed for the hire of slaves. Five other concurrent privileged debts dating from antebellum times remained unchanged.

fluence remained in the radical legislature, which in 1874 enacted a law allowing farmers, by written agreement, to "pledge or pawn" growing crops in return for advances necessary to produce the crop. The person advancing supplies or money had "a right of pledge upon the said crop, the same as if the said crop had been in the possession of the pledgee." The effect of this provision was to obligate a borrower to consign his crops to the merchant making the advances. A second section in the same law gave the merchant to whom the crops were consigned the right to pledge the crop—that is, he could borrow against a crop he did not own—and the right to sell the crop and "to appropriate the proceeds of sale to the payment to the amount due" for the advances he had made.[60]

The primary purpose of this law, like the earlier one, was to give postbellum factors and merchants the important commercial rights enjoyed by antebellum factors.[61] But postbellum laws extended these rights by imposing a legal obligation on the borrower to send his crops to the merchant who had provided the advances. The law protected landlords in a proviso that subordinated the merchant's claim to that "for the rent of the land on which the crop was produced."

Not until 1886 did the Louisiana legislature finally provide a clear ranking of all privileges. It continued to make the landlord's privilege for rent superior to that of merchants who had received written pledges as stipulated in the 1874 law and made both superior to that of "furnishers of supplies and of money." The distinction made in the law between a merchant who received a pledge in return for supplies and someone who merely furnished supplies reflected the distinction between the business of large New Orleans merchants and other suppliers. Large producers received advances to pay operating costs, including advances on wages, from the city factors in return for a "pledge" obligating them to consign the crop to be grown to the factors. If a tenant gave a pledge to a merchant and also took advances from the landlord, the landlord's privilege on the advances was subordinate to the pledge. Although it would appear, therefore, that Louisiana law did not pro-

60. Louisiana, *Acts, 1874* (March 21, 1874), 114–15.
61. The rights of factors and others to whom goods were consigned and/or pledged vitally affected their ability to borrow, discount notes, and protect any advances they had made. For a good discussion of these matters, see Richard Kilbourne, "Securing Commercial Transactions in the Antebellum Legal System of Louisiana," *Kentucky Law Journal,* 70 (1981–82), 609–641.

tect landlords' advances as fully as they were protected elsewhere, in practice there was little conflict on this score because large merchants would not deal with small tenant farmers. Landlords who leased small tracts and supplied their tenants had a safe privilege for rent and any advances they supplied their tenants. If the rent and repayment for advances due the landlord was a portion of the crop grown by the tenants, then the landlord could pledge this portion to a large city factor in order to get the advances that he could then pass on to his tenants.[62]

In the remaining southern states, the landlord's claim for his rent was more secure from the start than in Georgia, Mississippi, the Carolinas, and Louisiana because the first lien laws unambiguously subordinated the supplier's lien to that of the landlord for rent. Nevertheless, the laws in these states provided landlords with unwanted and potentially costly competition which, when they had the ability to do so, they moved to destroy.

Alabama's original 1866 lien law granted a lien to "any person" advancing supplies, but it protected the landlord's rent by stipulating that the supplier's lien "shall have preference of all other liens, except that for the rent of the land on which said crop may be made." When conflicts arose between merchants and landlords over advances, the radical legislature responded to landlord needs by amending the law in 1871 to give the landlord a superior lien for both rent and advances. Thus in Alabama, conservatives and radicals had given the landlords considerable protection long before the redeemer victory in 1874. As a result, the redeemers waited three years before making further changes in the lien laws.[63]

When the redeemers finally acted in 1877, they significantly increased both the landlord's protection from competing merchants and his ability to control his tenants. The 1866 law, as amended in 1871, provided that the advances which created a lien had to be "for the purpose of making a crop," and it listed those items that would qualify as necessary. The lien agreement had to be in writing and had to include a written statement by the borrower that "without such advance it would not be in the power of such person to procure the necessary team, provisions and farming implements, to make a

62. Louisiana, *Acts, 1886* (July 8, 1886), 127; Hewitt v. Williams, 47 Louisiana Ann. 742, 17 So. 269 (1895).
63. Alabama, *Acts, 1865–66* (January 15, 1866), 44; Alabama, *Acts, 1870–71* (March 8, 1871), 19.

crop." The listing of those items covered by the lien for advances created problems for all lenders, because the court ruled narrowly that the lien covered only those items specifically listed in the law.[64]

The new 1877 law significantly strengthened the landlord's position. It allowed the older laws to remain in force, except as they applied to landlords. The landlord retained his superior lien for rent and advances, but he no longer had to put his agreement in writing. In addition, the landlord's lien for advances included not only supplies (or money to buy supplies) to produce the crop, but also goods or money "for the sustenance or well being of the tenant or his family." This in effect defined anything the landlord advanced to his tenant as "necessary" to grow a crop and therefore covered by the landlord's lien. But because only landlord suppliers, not merchants, benefited from the new law's extended definition of "necessary" supplies, the new law made the landlord the preferred lender. His lien covered anything he advanced, but merchants who made advances often found that some of the items advanced did not come under the lien law as the court interpreted it.[65]

The landlord's lien for rent and advances extended to everything the tenant owned; it covered the crop to be grown and also "every article advanced" and "all property purchased with money so advanced or obtained by barter in exchange for any articles advanced." In addition, the new law allowed a landlord to carry an old debt over to a new year. If a tenant after turning over his crop and property remained in debt to his landlord and continued to rent the same land, the debt still due became a new lien on the following year's crop.

These provisions of the new law gave a landlord who so desired the ability to control all advances, including those personal items that affected the day-to-day well-being of his tenants, without fear of merchant competition. But the law also allowed the landlord, if he so desired, to avoid responsibilities for advances without endangering his claims for rent; he could "assign" his claims for advances to another "and the assignee shall be invested

64. Watson v. Auerbach, 57 Alabama 353 (1876).
65. Alabama, *Acts, 1876–77* (February 9, 1877), 74–77. For examples of interpretations of the law, see Schuessler v. Gains, 68 Alabama 556 (1881); Comer v. Daniel, 69 Alabama 434 (1881); Connor v. Jackson, 74 Alabama 464 (1883); Bell v. Hurst, 75 Alabama 44 (1883); Marcus v. Robinson, 76 Alabama 550 (1884); Beard v. Woodward, 78 Alabama 317 (1884); Boyett v. Potter, 80 Alabama 476, 2 So. 534 (1887).

with all the rights of the landlord."⁶⁶ In Alabama, as elsewhere, the landlord, not the tenant, decided if, and to whom, an assignment would be made.

Florida had provided landlords protection for rent during its territorial years, and in "An Act for the Relief of Landlords" in 1866 the conservative legislators continued that protection by providing the process by which a landlord could take possession of a defaulting tenant's crop and other property. Apparently Florida did not pass a separate crop lien law, although the 1866 law indicated that others might have a stake in the tenant's crop and other property and provided that the same process be followed by such creditors. The law did not specifically grant the landlord a lien, creating some uncertainties that the state supreme court in inconsistent rulings failed to resolve.⁶⁷

After the redeemers took control, they removed all uncertainties created by older legislation in a manner that significantly increased the landlord's rights. In 1879, the legislature repealed the 1866 law and in a new law gave the landlord a lien for rent on the tenant's crop and his other property and extended that lien to cover the crop and property of anyone who worked for the tenant. In 1881, the legislature expanded the landlord's superior lien to include any advances he had made. The law was clearly patterned on the Alabama law; its language was almost identical to that in Alabama's 1877 law. Also following the Alabama pattern was an 1885 statute that made it possible for an indebted tenant to lose almost everything he owned, including most of his private property: "no property

66. The landlord's superior lien for his rent remained in force even if he assigned his lien for advances to another, although if he guaranteed that the advancer would be repaid, he could lose his superior lien for rent. See Foster v. Napier, 74 Alabama 393 (1883). But the landlord could make an agreement with a merchant to supply his tenants and still reserve his lien for rent and, if he too provided supplies, he kept his lien for advances. Coleman v. Siler, 74 Alabama 435 (1883). Simply allowing a merchant to advance goods to a tenant with the "understanding" that he would be repaid by the tenant did not constitute an assignment of the landlord's lien for rent and advances, and the merchant would not receive a lien for the goods he advanced. Bell v. Hurst, 75 Alabama 44 (1883).

67. Florida, *Acts, 1828* (November 21, 1828), 201–203; Florida, *Acts, 1866* (January 16, 1866), 61–62. In Weed v. Standley, 12 Florida 166 (1868), the court ruled that the law "must be construed simply as enlarging and extending the remedy for the collection of rent, and does not give any lien upon the crops for rent." But in Patterson v. Taylor, 15 Florida 336 (1875), the court ruled that no lien existed "until a warrant for distress is issued according to the provisions of that act."

of any tenant or lessee shall be exempt from distress and sale for rent, except bed, bedclothes, and wearing apparel."[68]

Texas's first lien law in 1866 used language almost identical to the Alabama law of a few months earlier, granting a lien to suppliers that was superior to all others except rent and requiring that the agreement be in writing, recorded in the county courthouse, and contain a statement from the borrower that unless he received the supplies he could not make a crop. Under this law the landlord could be the supplier and therefore receive a lien for advances as well as for rent. But the Texas court, unlike that in Alabama, interpreted the law very broadly to the advantage of the landlord. In a case decided during the 1872–73 term, the supreme court ruled that a landlord had a superior lien for advances if his agreement to provide supplies preceded that of a merchant and the merchant received notice of the landlord's agreement with his tenant. Evidence in the case indicated that the landlord did not record his lien for supplies as required by the law, but that he had informed the merchant who later made an advance that the tenant had given him a lien for supplies and that he was providing such supplies. The court ruled that under these circumstances the failure to record the lien for advances was "immaterial" because the "only object of registration is to give notice of the existence and terms of the instrument so recorded."[69]

After 1874, Texas landlords no longer had to rely on sympathetic courts to protect their liens. The redeemer legislature that year repealed the 1866 law, along with laws dating from the 1840s concerning the landlord's lien for rent, and enacted new legislation that gave a superior lien to landlords for rent and any supplies they advanced without the requirement that the agreements be recorded. The courts imposed further limitations on the tenants, ruling that until the tenant paid his debt to the landlord, he could not remove any part of the crop, even if what remained was sufficient to pay the debt. Presumably, the repeal of the 1866 law meant that merchants could no longer secure a lien for advances, but this did not exclude merchants from dealings with the tenants if the landlord did not provide advances, assigned his lien for advances, or made an agreement with a merchant to supply his tenants.[70]

68. Florida, *Laws, 1879* (March 11, 1879), 72–74; Florida, *Acts, 1881* (February 22, 1881), 64; Florida, *Acts, 1885* (February 14, 1885), 26.

69. Texas, *Acts, 1866* (October 27, 1866), 64; McGee v. Fitzer, 37 Texas 27 (1872–73). See also Jones v. Avant, 41 Texas 650 (1874).

70. Texas, *Acts, 1874* (April 4, 1874), 55–59; Wilkes v. Adler and Others, 68 Texas 689, 5 S.W. 497 (1887).

Virginia, which never had a radical legislature, passed its first lien law later than the other southern states and provided the landlord with considerable protection from the start. Enacted in 1873, the law gave a lien on the crop to "any person or persons" who advanced "money or supplies" to "any person or persons" planting a crop. The agreement had to be in writing and recorded in the local county courthouse and was inferior to "the rights of landlords to their proper share of rents" and to any lien existing prior to the agreement. The landlord could easily protect any advances he proposed to give to any of his tenants by writing a lien agreement for such advances when he leased his land.[71]

Nevertheless, should a landlord fail to write and record a lien for advances or delay doing so, a merchant supplier could have a superior lien for advances to tenants whom the landlord might also have supplied. In early 1882, the legislature solved this potential problem by providing the landlord with a "prior" lien for all advances made to anyone cultivating his land and dropping the requirement that the landlord's lien for rent and advances be in writing. Merchants could still get a lien on a tenant's crop under the original law, which remained in force, but their lien was inferior to those of the landlord for both rent and advances, even if the merchant's lien predated that of the landlord.[72]

The Arkansas legislature in 1868 granted the landlord a lien on the crop grown for rent, but unlike other states, it did not provide a lien for supplies.[73] Landlords, tenants, and workers could get advances by giving a "mortgage" on what would become their portions of a future crop. Although this arrangement amply protected the landlord's rent—the court declared that a mortgage did not constitute a lien[74] and repeatedly ruled that a lien was superior to any mortgage[75]—landowners who advanced supplies to their tenants or workers might find that these same tenants or workers had mortgaged their crop to a merchant. This could prove especially dangerous to the

71. Virginia, *Acts, 1872–73* (April 2, 1873), 357–58.
72. Virginia, *Acts, 1881–82* (March 6, 1882), 239–40.
73. Arkansas, *Acts, 1868* (July 23, 1868), 245. The law did not require that the rental agreement be in writing in order to create a lien.
74. Franklin v. Meyer, 36 Arkansas 96 (1880).
75. Smith v. Myer and Bro., 25 Arkansas 609 (1869); Adams v. Hobbs, 27 Arkansas 1 (1871); Tomlinson v. Greenfield, 31 Arkansas 557 (1876); Lambeth v. Ponder, 33 Arkansas 707 (1878); Watson v. Johnson, 33 Arkansas 737 (1878); Buck v. Lee, 36 Arkansas 525 (1880); Meyer v. Bloom, 37 Arkansas 43 (1881).

landlord because the court narrowly construed the landlord's lien for rent to cover only payment for the use of the land and not for the use of any stock, equipment, or other items the landlord provided.[76]

In 1885, the legislature gave the landlord additional protection by making his advances to tenants and workers a lien, "which lien shall have preference over any mortgage or other conveyance of such crop made by such tenant or employe [sic]." The new law defined the advances covered as "necessary supplies, either of money, provisions, clothing, stock, or other necessary articles." The court construed the word "necessary" very broadly, ruling that the articles furnished need not be of "direct use" in growing the crop in order to be under the lien; it accepted as necessary supplies such items as a cow to provide milk for the family, a sewing machine to make clothing, and medicines and doctor bills.[77] Like similar laws elsewhere, this legislation gave the Arkansas landlord clear dominance over his tenants, allowing him to give or withhold "necessary articles" as he wished without fear of merchant interference. But the laws did not foreclose all opportunities for merchants. The landlord was not required to advance supplies to his tenants, and he could, if he so desired, waive his lien for supplies and choose a particular merchant to supply his tenants.[78]

Tennessee as early as 1825 gave the landlord a superior lien for rent on his tenant's crops, a law that remained unchanged in the postbellum era.[79] Suppliers could get a mortgage (rather than a lien) until 1870, when the legislature provided suppliers with a lien for advances, the lien being inferior to that for rent but superior to any mortgages. The lien for supplies had to

76. Varner v. Rice, 39 Arkansas 344 (1882); Roth v. Williams, 45 Arkansas 447 (1885).

77. Arkansas, *Acts, 1885* (April 6, 1885), 225; Earl Bros. & Co. v. Malone, 80 Arkansas 218, 96 S.W. 1062 (1906). See also Airey v. Weinstein, 54 Arkansas 443, 16 S.W. 123 (1891); Bourland *et al.* v. McKnight & Bro., 79 Arkansas 427, 96 S.W. 179 (1906); Ferniman v. Nowlin, 91 Arkansas 20, 120 S.W. 378 (1909).

78. Tinsley v. Craige, 54 Arkansas 346, 16 S.W. 570 (1891); Bigham v. Cropss, 69 Arkansas 581, 65 S.W. 101 (1901).

79. Section 3539 in the 1858 Tennessee *Code* (the last codification before the Civil War): "Any debt by note, account or otherwise, created for the rent of land, is a lien on the crop growing or made on the premises, in preference to all other debts, from the date of the contract." In 1871, when the state published *Public Statutes of the State of Tennessee, Since the Year 1858... A Supplement to the Code,* it contained no indication that the earlier law was amended or repealed. See pp. 267–71. See also Schoenlau-Steiner Trunk Top & Veneer Co. v. Hilderbrand *et al.*, 152 Tennessee 166, 274 S.W. 544 (1925).

be in writing. Legislation in 1875 strengthened the landowner's position by extending his superior lien for rent to include advances and removing the requirement that the landlord's lien for supplies be in writing.[80]

In every southern state, the former planters who controlled the first postbellum legislatures expected the crop lien laws to provide them with the credit they needed and in so doing to help them solve what they called the "labor problem" by allowing them to transform their former slaves into dependent hired labor. Freedmen would become employees who would continue to work in gangs under the direction of the planter or his overseer, and planter-employers, by providing a lien on the crop to be grown, could get needed supplies and equipment along with food, clothing, and other necessities that they would distribute to their workers as advances on their wages. By delaying final wage payments until the end of the year and by promising that the workers' wages would be a share of the crop they produced, the landowners sought to achieve a maximum of season-long control of their work force with a minimum of working capital. Master-slave relations would become employer-employee relations with the fewest possible alterations in both the organization of production and control of the work force. Such was the planters' dream.

But the planters' dream was the freedmen's nightmare, since returning to traditional relationships was exactly what they sought to avoid. As their hopes of getting land of their own to gain independence from their former owners faded, freedmen discovered other ways to achieve at least a measure of that independence. They found that merchants would provide them with goods in return for a crop lien on their wages, that is, on their share of the

---

80. Tennessee, *Laws, 1870* (January 12, 1870), 191; Hughes v. Whitaker, 51 Tennessee 399 (1871); Whitmore v. Poindexter, 66 Tennessee 248 (1874); Tennessee, *Laws, 1875* (March 23, 1875), 206. The *Tennessee Code, 1884,* p. 818, explained that this law "was intended to give the lien for supplies furnished without the writing required by the act of 1870." The law required merely that the landlord keep an account of such advances. The *Code, 1896,* p. 1348, repeated much the same statement and noted that the account could be in any form, "even on a loose sheet of paper," so long as the landlord swore it was made at the time the advances were given. But a new annotation to the law limited the lien to the supply of "necessary supplies of food and clothing." If the landlord supplied equipment and workstock, he had to list these items in writing in order to get a lien. See also Dunlap v. Aycock, 57 Tennessee 561 (1873); Thurman v. Jenkins, 61 Tennessee 426 (1873); Lewis v. Mahon, 68 Tennessee 374 (1878).

crop to be grown. Ironically, the crop lien laws of 1866–67, designed by planter-dominated legislatures to provide the financial backing necessary to create a dependent labor force, became the means for the workers, with alternative sources of advances from merchants, to escape that dependence.

When the resistance of the freedmen to work in gangs in the antebellum pattern led planters to divide their plantations into small units, allowing self-generated squads of freedmen[81] or, more commonly, individual families to work particular tracts, their wages being a share of the output of the particular tracts they worked, the landlords' problems increased. Many, faced with persisting pressure from the freedmen and unable or unwilling to cope with dealing with free labor, allowed the operators of these small tracts to become tenants who paid their rent in the form of a share of the crop produced. When this happened, the original lien laws became even more menacing to the landlords as liens given by tenants to merchants threatened to take the crops pledged for rent and/or any advances the landlords had made.

Although the amount of legal protection enjoyed by landlords differed somewhat from state to state, in every state that protection proved inadequate, at least from the landlords' point of view, and as long as the radicals remained in power, the landlords usually received little help from the legislatures and the courts. Even in those states where the landlords enjoyed a superior lien for their rent, they had little or no guarantee that they would be paid for any supplies they advanced to their tenants.

The redeemers, however, were far more sympathetic than the radicals to the plight of the planters. Once in power, they changed the lien laws to solve the unforeseen problems that had arisen under the original laws that the Johnsonian reconstruction governments had so quickly passed. Landlords received the protection they desired at the expense of the merchants when new legislation gave landlords liens for rent and advances that were superior to all other liens and could arise and be legally enforceable from a simple oral agreement. By subordinating the merchants' claims to those of the landlords, the new laws weakened competition for the tenants' business,

81. Ralph Shlomowitz discusses the short-lived squad system in two essays: "The Origins of Southern Sharecropping," *Agricultural History,* LIII (July, 1979), 557–75, and "The Squad System on Postbellum Cotton Plantations," in *Towards a New South? Studies in Post-Civil War Southern Communities,* eds. Orville Vernon Burton and Robert C. McMath (Westport, Conn., 1982), 265–80.

thereby giving landlords considerably more authority over their tenants.

These severe limitations on the merchants did not force them out of the black belt and into the hill country, as some have suggested.[82] Many remained and continued to serve the landlords much as they had before the war, providing (as the prewar factors had done) supplies to the landlords, who then passed these supplies on to their tenants. In such cases, the landlord had a lien on the crops of his tenants for rent and supplies, but the merchant received a lien on the landlord's crop, that is, on the crop he would receive as rent and repayment for supplies advanced. If the superiority of the landlord's liens for rent and supplies increased the risk for merchants who might deal directly with tenants, they had ample business from landlords who wanted to supply their tenants but lacked adequate resources of their own.

The increase in the number of stores and the rise of the furnishing merchant system in the hill country populated largely by white landowners and a rapidly growing number of tenants occurred because of increased business opportunities as farmers in these areas moved into commercial production. Hill country farmers also needed credit, and the expansion of cotton and tobacco acreage in these areas attracted merchants who provided supplies, consumers' goods, marketing facilities, and credit.[83]

When merchants dealt with landowners, both in the hill country and in the old plantation areas, they often demanded, in addition to the lien on the crop, a mortgage on the landlord's property, including his land. The po-

---

82. According to Jonathan M. Wiener, the new lien laws caused the merchants to shift "towards the white yeomen areas outside the black belt, where they could continue to take crop liens without fear that the debtors' crops would go to planters instead of themselves." Wiener, "Planter-Merchant Conflict in Reconstruction Alabama," *Past & Present,* No. 68 (August, 1975), 88.

83. In 1900, the first time the census collected data on tenure of farm operators by race, it reported that 36 percent of the white farm operators in the South were tenants, and the number of white tenant farm operators exceeded those run by blacks by almost 30 percent. (U. S. Bureau of the Census, *Agriculture, 1954,* Vol. II [Washington, 1956], 954–55). Harold D. Woodman, *King Cotton and His Retainers: Financing and Marketing the Cotton Crop of the South, 1800–1925* (Lexington, 1968), 295–314; Roger L. Ransom and Richard Sutch, *One Kind of Freedom: The Economic Consequences of Emancipation* (Cambridge, 1977), 120–25, 132–37, 140–46; Thomas D. Clark, *Pills, Petticoats and Plows: The Southern Country Store* (Indianapolis, 1944); Thomas D. Clark, "The Furnishing and Supply System in Southern Agriculture Since 1865," *Journal of Southern History,* XII (February, 1946), 24–44; Steven Hahn, *The Roots of Southern Populism: Yeoman Farmers and the Transformation of the Georgia Upcountry, 1850–1890* (New York, 1983), 170–203.

tential cost to the landowner could be devastating, for if the crop did not suffice to pay his debt to the merchant, the landowner could lose some or even all of his land and become himself a tenant, renting land he once owned from a merchant who now became a landowner protected by the revised lien laws.[84] The growing number of white tenants and the vehement attacks on merchants and the crop lien system that were central features of the alliance and populist movements indicate that the danger was real.

If some merchants became landlords, they also retained the trade of tenants renting from others, despite the subordination of their liens to those of landlords, because some landlords preferred to lease their land and allow their tenants to make their own arrangements for supplies. The revised lien laws allowed a landlord to assign his superior lien for supplies to a merchant and still retain his superior lien for rent, making it possible for him to become an absentee earning rental income without the trouble, expense, and risk of providing his tenants with advances.[85]

But if the new lien laws allowed landlords to become absentee rentiers, they also permitted those with the resources and the desire to do so to exercise considerable control over their rented lands. Although traditional law concerning landlord-tenant relations gave the tenant control of the property he rented, subject only to his obligation to pay the agreed-upon rent and to maintain the rented property, the lien laws enacted by the redeemers allowed a landlord who desired to do so to make a tenant completely dependent, relying upon his landowner not only for the land he worked but also for day-to-day living expenses that the landlord could give or withhold in order to maintain close supervision of his tenant's work.

In some areas, however, the freedmen, even when they forced landowners to grant them individual plots to work, never became tenants. Instead,

---

84. See Woodman, *King Cotton and His Retainers,* 312; Ransom and Sutch, *One Kind of Freedom,* 147.

85. This arrangement could prove dangerous, as many landowners discovered. Merchants called upon to provide advances to tenants would seek to limit their risk by demanding additional security from landlords. The laws allowed them to require that the landlord waive all or part of his lien for rent, which made the merchant's lien superior to the extent of the amount waived: See Georgia, *Acts, 1875,* 20; Alabama, *Acts, 1876–77,* 75; Foxworth v. Brown *et al.*, 120 Alabama 59, 24 So. 1 (1898); Newman *et al.* v. Bank of Greenville *et al.*, 66 Mississippi 323, 5 So. 753 (1889); Dreyfus *et al.* v. W. A. Gage & Co., 84 Mississippi 219, 36 So. 248 (1904). They could also demand a mortgage on the landlord's land as added security for the tenant's debt.

they became sharecroppers. Although the Census Bureau listed them as tenants, the sharecroppers—or croppers, as they were more commonly called in the South—were legally considered to be workers, their wages being a specific portion of what they produced.[86] This tenure form, essentially a continuation of the share-wages system without many of its gang-labor features, is the subject of the next chapter.

86. Historians have consistently erred by considering sharecropping to be merely a special form of tenancy. For a recent example, see Ransom and Sutch, *One Kind of Freedom,* 87–94. A major source of the historians' confusion is that the Bureau of the Census, one of the most commonly used historical sources, consistently confused the two tenure forms. Not until 1880 did the census differentiate tenants from owners in the general category of farm operators, dividing tenants into those who paid a money rental and those who paid a share of the produce as rent. The census did not even designate the category of cropper until 1920, and then it (incorrectly) listed the cropper as a special form of tenant found exclusively in the South. Because tenants often paid their rent in the form of a share of the crops they grew, share tenancy had a superficial resemblance to sharecropping. Furthermore, as we shall see, the language used by contemporaries, including the courts, could sometimes be misleading. Such problems in the sources have caused many historians to fail to see the difference between the two tenure forms. Nevertheless, most southerners and certainly the courts were well aware of the differences—and their significance.

CHAPTER THREE

"An Obvious Distinction Between a Cropper and a Tenant"
The Legal Status of Landlords, Croppers, and Tenants

William Alexander Percy, lawyer, intellectual, and cotton planter, in his 1941 autobiography, *Lanterns on the Levee*, called the 149 families who worked on "Trail Lake," his 3,300-acre plantation in the Mississippi Delta, "workers" who were his "partners" participating in a "profit-sharing" plan. In the space of a few pages, however, he also called these profit-sharing worker-partners "tenants" and "peasants." One term Percy did not use was *share-cropper*. He knew that the propertyless workers on his plantation "worked 'on the shares' and called themselves 'croppers,'" but he denied being familiar with the term *share-cropper* as it was used in the northern press. "I woke to the discovery that in pseudo-intellectual circles from Moscow to Santa Monica the Improvers-of-the world had found something new in the South to shudder over." In language that echoed the proslavery arguments of a century earlier, Percy attacked critics for failing to understand that the profit-sharing arrangement on his and other plantations was "the most moral system under which human beings can work together" and that "if it were accepted in principle by capital and labor, our industrial troubles would largely cease."[1]

---

1. William Alexander Percy, *Lanterns on the Levee: Recollections of a Planter's Son* (1941; rpr. Baton Rouge, 1973), 278–81. The blacks working on his plantation, he wrote, "are simple unskilled laborers. I wonder what other unskilled labor for so little receives so much. Plantations do not close down during the year and there's no firing, because partners can't fire one another. Our plantation system seems to me to offer as humane, just, self-respect-

Percy was disingenuous in claiming to be unfamiliar with the term *sharecropper*. Southerners seldom used the word, but they did use the term *cropper* both in ordinary language and in the official language of legislation and judicial proceedings. More important than the word used, however, was its specific legal meaning, which Percy, the Delta plantation owner who surely knew better, buried in his apologia. Those who worked at "Trail Lake" were not his partners who shared in the profits of his plantation, nor were they peasants or tenants. They were wage workers whose wages were a share of what they produced, or more typically, their wages were a share of the *proceeds* of what they produced.

Long before Percy wrote, lawmakers in every southern state had clearly defined what a *cropper* was, and they sharply and unambiguously distinguished between a tenant (whatever the form of his rental payment — money, a set amount of the crop grown, or a share of the crop) and a cropper. "There is an obvious distinction between a cropper and a tenant," declared the Georgia Supreme Court in an 1872 decision. "The case of the cropper is rather a mode of paying wages than a tenancy," the court explained. A year earlier, a Tennessee court had made the same distinction: "an agreement on the part of one who is to do the labor, to take charge of and manage the land on shares, is not regarded as a lease but more in the nature of payment for services rendered, by a part of the crops raised." The courts in every southern state came to the same conclusion: the cropper was a wage laborer, his wages being a portion of what he produced paid *to* him *by* the landlord. The tenant was a renter who paid rent *to* the landlord for use of the land; it did not alter that relationship if the rent was a portion of the crop produced.[2]

Until the middle of the twentieth century, when cropping was rapidly

---

ing, and cheerful a method of earning a living as human beings are likely to devise." He went on in a manner reminiscent of George Fitzhugh to contrast the lives of his happy "partners" with the sad plight of workers elsewhere. "I watch the limber-jointed, oily-black, well-fed, decently clothed peasants on Trail Lake and feel sorry for the telephone girls, the clerks in chain stores, the office help, the unskilled laborers everywhere—not only for their poor and fixed wage but for their slave routine, their joyless habits of work, and their insecurity." Ibid., 280.

2. Appling v. Odom and Mercier, 46 Georgia 583 (1872); Mann v. Taylor, 52 Tennessee 267 (1871). See also Christian v. Crocker *et al.*, 25 Arkansas 327 (1869); Bres & O'Brien v. S. C. & J. A. Cowan, 22 Louisiana Ann. 438 (1870); Hunt v. Wing *et al.*, 57 Tennessee 139 (1872); Betts v. Ratliff, 50 Mississippi 561 (1874); Huff v. Watkins, 15 South Carolina 82

disappearing,³ the courts consistently drew a sharp distinction between the tenant and the cropper. And for good reason: the two tenure forms entailed significant differences in the rights and obligations of the parties involved — the landowner, the tiller of the soil, and any lender of supplies and money. Litigation on the matter continued to appear before southern courts, not because litigants questioned the principle of the difference between a cropper and a tenant, but rather because they disagreed over whether a particular written or oral agreement created a landlord-tenant or a landlord-cropper relationship.⁴

Oral agreements were informal and notoriously vague, but even writ-

---

(1880); Parrish v. Commonwealth, 81 Virginia 1 (1884); McGee v. Fitzer, 37 Texas 27 (1872–73); Moore et al. v. Linn et al., 19 Oklahoma 279, 91 P. 910 (1907); State v. Burwell, 63 North Carolina 661 (1869).

3. Sharecropping of a very different kind continues to exist in some areas. Retired farmers, inheritors of land who choose not to work it, and investors make agreements with local farmers to share expenses and returns on land and call the arrangement "sharecropping," but the legal relations are more in the nature of a partnership, which, as we shall see, the cropping arrangement was not, and the size of the tracts of land involved are usually very large.

4. In addition to the cases already cited above, see the following as examples among many: Ponder v. Rhea, 32 Arkansas 435 (1877); Sentell v. Moore, 34 Arkansas 687 (1879); Hammock v. Creekmore, 48 Arkansas 264, 3 S.W. 180 (1887); Bourland et al. v. McKnight & Bros., 79 Arkansas 427, 96 S.W. 179 (1906); Johnson v. Mantooth, 108 Arkansas 36, 156 S.W. 448 (1913); Barnhardt v. State, 169 Arkansas 567, 275 S.W. 909 (1925); Almond v. Scott, 80 Georgia 95, 4 S.E. 892 (1888); McElmurray v. Turner, 86 Georgia 212, 12 S.E. 358 (1890); DeLoach et al. v. Delk, 119 Georgia 884, 47 S.E. 204 (1904); Fields v. Harris, 34 Georgia App. 445, 129 S.E. 664 (1925); Lalanne Brothers v. McKinney, 28 Louisiana Ann. 642 (1876); Holmes v. Payne, 4 Louisiana App. 345 (1926); Jones v. Dowling, 12 Louisiana App. 362, 125 So. 478 (1929); Lumbley v. Thomas, 65 Mississippi 97, 5 So. 823 (1887); Alexander v. Zeigler, 84 Mississippi 560, 36 So. 536 (1894); Carpenter v. Strickland, 20 South Carolina 1 (1883); McCutchen v. Cranshaw et al., 40 South Carolina 511, 19 S.E. 140 (1894); Malcolm Mercantile Co. v. Britt, 102 South Carolina 499, 87 S.E. 143 (1915); People's Bank v. Walker, 132 South Carolina 254, 128 S.E. 715 (1925); Horsley v. Moss et al., 5 Texas C.A. 341, 23 S.W. 1115 (1893); Turner v. First National Bank of Sulphur Springs, Texas C.A., 234 S.W. 928 (1921); Brown v. Johnson, 118 Texas 143, 12 S.W. (2d.) 543 (1929). The distinction assumed national importance in the application of New Deal agricultural policies in the South. See A. B. Book, "A Note on the Legal Status of Share-Tenants and Share-Croppers in the South," *Law and Contemporary Problems*, IV (October, 1937), 539. Book was a member of the legal staff of the Agricultural Adjustment Administration (AAA) during the New Deal. When planters argued that croppers were not entitled to tenants' benefits and protection under the AAA, Book was instructed to study the relevant law for the agency. His typewritten memoranda, which led me into some of the relevant case reports, may be found in Record

ten contracts often failed to state clearly and precisely the kind of relationship being created or used language that might be variously interpreted. Planters, tenants, and croppers reserved the term *wages* to mean money wages, which left them no term for the wages in kind paid croppers, and especially in the early years when the cropper system was becoming established, they often used terms such as *rent* and *lease* when the ordinary meaning—to say nothing of the strictly legal meaning—of such terms was not intended. Even lawyers and judges regularly used these words imprecisely. Such confusion led to disagreements over what kind of relationship an oral or written contract had created, making the court's interpretation crucial in determining the ownership of property under dispute. An early decision in Georgia, already quoted in part, illustrates both the nature and sources of disagreements and the significance for those involved of the courts' decisions resolving these disagreements.

The case involved a dispute between A. J. Mercier, an Early County landowner, and Thomas K. Appling, a merchant. Named in the case, but neither present at the hearings nor directly involved in the outcome, was Stephen Odom.[5] In 1871, Odom, along with John Mozee, contracted with Mercier to produce crops on Mercier's land. Sometime during the year, Odom incurred a debt with Appling, providing a promissory note secured by a mortgage on the crop of corn and cotton he was raising on Mercier's land. When Odom failed to pay the note, Appling foreclosed on the mortgage, and in December, the local court ordered that five bales of cotton alleged to be the property of Odom be taken to satisfy the debt. In early February, 1872, Mercier, the landowner, filed a claim on this cotton, arguing that it belonged to him and not to Odom, and therefore it had been improperly seized. The case was tried before a jury in the superior court of Early County. In his instructions to the jury, the judge declared that Appling (the merchant) could take the cotton only if Mercier "had divided the cotton and set it apart as the property of Stephen Odom."

The superior court judge's charge to the jury assumed that the contract between Mercier and Odom had been one of landlord and cropper, which meant that the crop produced was Mercier's until he divided it and gave

---

Group 16, Records of the Office of the Secretary of Agriculture, General Correspondence, Office of the General Counsel, AAA, File 466—Landlord-Tenant, National Archives, Washington, D.C.

5. Appling v. Odom and Mercier, 46 Georgia 583 (1872).

Odom his share; that is, the entire crop belonged to the employer until he paid his worker his wages. If Mercier had not made the division, the entire crop remained his property, and therefore it could not be seized to satisfy Odom's debt.[6] The judge did not leave it to the jury to determine the nature of the contract; the jury was merely to decide on the basis of the evidence presented whether Odom, the cropper, had been paid his share by his employer, Mercier, before the cotton had been seized. When the jury, following the judge's instructions, sided with Mercier, Appling appealed on the grounds that the judge's instructions had been improper.

In its decision, the Georgia Supreme Court outlined the facts of the case using language to describe the contract that made it appear to be a tenancy: "A. J. Mercier was to furnish the land and mules, and Mozee and Odom to furnish the labor to make a crop; . . . A. J. Mercier was to have one-half the crop for his rent."[7] Despite its use of the term *rent*, which clearly suggested that Odom was a tenant, the supreme court agreed with the judge of the lower court that the contract made Odom a cropper, not a tenant. Because, the court explained, the cropper is merely a wage laborer, "the title of the crop subject to the wages is in the owner of the land." Therefore, the supreme court concluded in sustaining the lower court's judgment in favor of Mercier, the merchant could not touch what might become the cropper's crop until the employer had actually given it to him. In its decision, the supreme court carefully described the distinction between a cropper and a tenant, but this was not the real issue in the case. Rather, the case turned on how the court would interpret the contract, for if it had determined that Odom had been a tenant, the court admitted, "a different rule might obtain."

Because the court had ruled that Odom was not a tenant, it did not consider what that "different rule" might be, but obviously Appling's attorney believed it would benefit his client. Had Odom been a tenant, he would have had ownership of the crop until he divided it, that is, until he paid his rent and whatever he owed for advances. In Georgia in 1872, the priority of the liens for rent and for advances from the landowner and the merchant was

---

6. Of course, the worker had a right to his wages—in this instance, a share of the crop—but the payment of wages was not at issue in the case because Odom owed his entire share to the landlord and the merchant.

7. Other evidence indicated that Mercier had furnished Mozee and Odom with supplies "to be paid for before the crop was to be removed from the place."

still unclear. If Odom was a tenant and if the landlord's agreements with him were not in writing and did not predate the agreement with the merchant, the merchant may have been legally in the right in seizing the crop.[8] This explains why the merchant's lawyer objected to the instructions to the jury by the judge of the lower court that indicated that he found Odom to be a cropper, not a tenant. When the supreme court agreed with the lower court's determination that Odom was a cropper, the merchant lost his claim to the crop.

The evidence supporting the court's decision was ambiguous. The contract did not specifically term Odom a cropper, and the court, adding to the ambiguity, used the term *rent* in outlining the evidence before it. Nevertheless, it concluded that the contract did not create a tenancy.

Similar ambiguities appeared in other decisions. In an Arkansas case, for example, the court described an agreement in which a landowner, Rhea, "let Johnson, in 1874, have twenty acres of ground, in his plantation, to cultivate that year, in corn and cotton."[9] Johnson agreed that the landlord would retain possession of the crop produced until Johnson delivered enough of it to pay "for the rent of the land," the cost of advances, and a debt of $100, Johnson "to have what remained." Johnson later in the year received supplies from Ponder, a merchant, and provided Ponder with "a mortgage upon the crop, except so much as was due for rent." When the cotton and corn matured but had not yet been harvested, Johnson sold the crop to the merchant to satisfy his mortgage, whereupon the landlord "gathered the crop, and refused to let him [the merchant] have any portion of it." Ponder then sued Rhea for "trespass, in taking and converting to his own use 4000 pounds of seed cotton and 200 bushels of corn." When the Lawrence County Circuit Court sided with the landowner and allowed him to keep the crop, the merchant appealed.

In its decision affirming the lower court's judgment, the Arkansas Supreme Court concluded that Johnson was a cropper because, it explained, "there is no evidence that it was the intention that the relation of landlord and tenant should exist" between the "lessor" and the "cultivator." Thus, even though the court had used the term *rent* in describing the worker's obligations under the contract and had referred to the landlord as a "lessor"

8. See chapter 2, pp. 28–32.
9. Ponder v. Rhea, 32 Arkansas 435 (1877). The court did not use the given names of the parties to the dispute.

in its decision, it nevertheless decided that Johnson was a cropper, not a tenant, and therefore the entire crop belonged to the employer.

The key word in the decision was the court's determination of the "intention" of the parties involved. The courts reserved to themselves the right to decide which relationship existed when the evidence was not entirely obvious. The courts had to interpret the "intent" of the contracting parties, declared the North Carolina Supreme Court when, in an 1874 decision, it considered evidence similar to that in the Georgia and Arkansas cases but came to an opposite conclusion.[10] A superior court in Nash County had decided that a particular contract had created a landlord-cropper relationship, and therefore the cropper, although he had entered into a written crop lien agreement with a merchant who provided supplies, had "no title to the cotton ... and ... consequently no right to convey any title" to the merchant. The supreme court, to whom the merchant appealed, agreed that the lower court was correct in making the distinction between a cropper and a tenant, but it ruled that the lower court had erred in finding the cultivator to be a cropper. Although the "difference between a tenant and a cropper is clear," the court declared, deciding whether a particular agreement between an "occupier" of the land and the landowner created a tenant or cropper relationship was not always obvious. "It is a question of interpretation, and the intent, when ascertained, must govern, as in other contracts."

Determining intent was no easy task, the court admitted, especially when contracts were oral or badly written. Even "the use of the word 'rent,' as that the owner has 'rented' his land to another, has, by itself, but little weight in the interpretation of an oral or inartificially [sic] and obscurely written contract." To make its interpretation, the court must look to other evidence in "the agreement between the parties." In this case, the contract was oral, but because the cultivator had testified that he had agreed to "give" the landlord half the crop for rent, the court concluded that the intent of the contract was to create a tenancy. In this, as in other cases, the court's determination that the agreement created a tenancy had significant results. Because North Carolina law in 1871 gave the landlord a lien for rent and advances only if he put his agreement in writing, the merchant's written contract created a lien that took precedence over the landlord's claims under his oral agreement with his tenant.[11]

10. Harrison v. Ricks, 71 North Carolina 7 (1874).
11. See chapter 2, pp. 51–53.

The landlord-cropper relationship was not based on new legislation in the postbellum South, nor was it the result of judge-made law arbitrarily imposed by postemancipation courts intent on protecting landowner interests. On the contrary, long before the Civil War, in both the North and the South, the courts had drawn the distinction between a tenant and a cropper and provided ample legal precedents to establish that the landlord-cropper relation was one between employer and employee governed by the common law and statutes concerning master and servant or employer and employee relations. Early nineteenth-century disputes that led to litigation, like those that arose later, turned on the intentions of parties to an agreement and did not question that a cropper agreement created an employer-employee relationship and not a tenancy.[12] With ample legal precedents available, specific legislation defining the landlord-cropper relationship was unnecessary.

In only two southern states, North Carolina and Alabama, did the postbellum legislatures enact laws defining the relationship, and in both the ultimate intent was not to create it but to abolish it. The courts in North Carolina, adhering to early precedents, continued to make the distinction between tenants and croppers in the early postwar years, but in 1877, in an amendment to the "Landlord and Tenant Act" (of 1869), the legislature abolished the distinction; thereafter, both tenants and croppers were deemed to be croppers.[13] Alabama, unlike the other states, enacted legislation in 1877 that clearly defined the distinction between croppers and tenants, but this

---

12. For example, in 1829 the Pennsylvania Supreme Court considered a case in which one of the lawyers contended that "the plaintiff was not a tenant, but a servant, or agent, working on the shares." The court ruled that the evidence did not support the lawyer's claim, but it accepted the principle of a distinction between a tenant and a cropper, and took the occasion to describe the difference. It explained that "renting for a share of the produce of a farm" was common in Pennsylvania, and such an arrangement created a tenancy. This share tenancy, the court continued, created the "difficulty" of "confounding a cropper with a tenant," but the two were not the same. A share tenant paid a share of what he produced to the landlord for rent; the cropper was merely a laborer. "If one hires a man to work his farm, and gives him a share of the produce, he is a cropper. He has no interest in the land, but receives his share as the price of his labour." Fry v. Jones, 2 Rawle (Pennsylvania) 11 (1829). Antebellum courts in the South came to the same conclusion: State v. Jones, 19 North Carolina 544 (1837); Brazier v. Ansley, 33 North Carolina 12 (1850); Denton v. Strickland, 48 North Carolina 61 (1855); Smith v. Tankersley, 20 Alabama 213 (1852), and the cases cited therein.

13. State v. Burwell, 63 North Carolina 661 (1869); Wolston v. Bryan, 64 North Carolina 764 (1870); Harrison v. Ricks, 71 North Carolina 7 (1874); North Carolina, *Laws, 1876–77*

did not spare the courts from considerable litigation on the matter where the issue, as in other states, was which relationship a particular agreement created. Finally, in a revision of the legal code in 1923, the codifiers omitted provisions concerning the landlord-cropper relation, and the courts thereafter ruled that the omission abolished the landlord-cropper relation and made croppers as well as true tenants into tenants.[14]

If the cropper relationship did not originate in the postbellum South and if it did not completely disappear in the North, it became almost solely a southern institution after the Civil War. The 1920 Census, which belatedly for the first time recognized the existence of croppers, considered it to be peculiar to the South, listing statistics for croppers only for the southern states.[15]

The landlord-cropper relationship became widespread and important in the South in response to conflicts generated by emancipation. When former slaves resisted working in gangs under supervision and landowners agreed to assign them family-sized tracts on which to work, some landlords, unwilling or unable to cope with the exigencies of directing a free labor force, allowed the operators of the small tracts to become tenants. As we have seen, the tenants, aided by the lien laws and merchants eager for business, sought to extend the relative autonomy that tenancy allowed, and the landlords discovered that they had inadequate guarantees for their rent and any advances they gave to their tenants. New tenancy laws allowed a landowner to lease his lands and exercise only casual or intermittent supervision of his tenants without fear that his tenants' other creditors might absorb his rent and any advances he might have supplied.

Some landowners, however, wanted to continue to exercise close supervision of the work on their lands. Although most were unable to rein-

---

(March 12, 1877), 551–54. A perceptive discussion of the evolution of the law in North Carolina is Marjorie Mendenhall Applewhite, "Sharecropper and Tenant in the Courts of North Carolina," *North Carolina Historical Review*, XXXI (April, 1954), 134–49.

14. Alabama, *Code, 1923,* Section 8807; Stewart v. Young, 212 Alabama 426, 103 So. 44 (1925); Heaton v. Slaton *et al.,* 141 So. 267 (Alabama, 1932). See also the discussion of the matter in Alabama, *Code, 1928,* Section 8807.

15. U.S. Bureau of Census, *Fourteenth Census, 1920: Agriculture,* 124, and Table 14. For examples of the cropper relationship in the North, see Adams v. McKeeson, 53 Pennsylvania St. 81 (1866); Steel v. Frick, 56 Pennsylvania St. 172 (1867); Porter v. Chandler, 27 Minnesota 301 (1880).

troduce a gang labor system, they discovered that the division of their lands into small family-sized tracts could be a minor, if unwanted, concession. The cropper relation allowed such landowners to assign workers a particular tract to cultivate and to pay them a portion of what they produced as wages while still retaining managerial power and at the same time lessening the danger of conflicting claims on the croppers' wages. Because the croppers were simply wage laborers paid in kind, the landowner-employer retained managerial control, and like any employer of wage labor, although he was obligated to pay his workers their wages, he owned the product of their labor. Before paying his croppers their shares — that is, their wages — the landlord simply deducted the cost of any advances he had made. Only then could other creditors seek reimbursement from the cropper.

This arrangement did not emerge full-blown from the start. Not only did landowner-merchant contention arise over the nature of the contract between the landowner and those who worked his land, but the croppers themselves sought to give a very different meaning to the landowner-cropper relationship. When disputes led to litigation, the courts, while consistently reiterating the distinction between a tenant and a cropper,[16] also spelled out the rights and duties of croppers, basing their rulings on available precedents and on new statutes. In each of the southern states, croppers, like tenants, saw many of their rights erode, especially after the landowners reasserted their power following the departure of the Freedmen's Bureau and the fall of the radical regimes.

Some of the early cases in which the courts described the legal distinction between the tenant and the cropper came in response to efforts by some blacks to challenge the power of their former owners by giving their own interpretation to the landowner-cropper relationship. They insisted that when the landowner provided the land and equipment and the freedmen provided the labor, the relationship was neither that of employer and employee nor of landlord and tenant, but rather a partnership. This arrangement, had it been accepted, would have been almost as revolutionary as land confiscation and redistribution, for although the landowner partner might retain ownership of the land, decisions on the use of the land, work regimes, the crops to be grown, sales, and the distribution of any profits—in short, all management decisions—would be shared by the partners.

16. As already noted above, two states, North Carolina and Alabama, abolished the distinction between croppers and tenants.

The courts quickly and unequivocally dismissed all such contentions by the croppers. The cropper relationship "does not constitute a partnership," declared the Arkansas Supreme Court in 1869, "it simply establishes a rule whereby . . . labor is to be compensated." A Louisiana court agreed. The landowners, it declared in an 1870 case, "employed certain laborers and agreed to give them, in lieu of wages, one-third the gross product of cotton. There was plainly no partnership in this." The cropper was an employee, ruled a South Carolina court, and "the fact that . . . the compensation of the laborer is not a fixed and definite sum of money, but is made to depend upon the amount of the proceeds of his labor" did not alter his status and "certainly" did not create a partnership with his employer. The courts in other states ruled in much the same way whenever the question of partnership arose.[17]

If the cropper was neither a tenant nor a partner but rather a wage laborer, he had a right to his wages, which gave him a direct interest in the crop from which he would receive his share or at least the proceeds of his share, even if that interest did not give him either management rights or ownership and control. But the worker's right to a share as his wages often conflicted with the rights of landowners, tenants, or merchants who might have an interest in the same crop. At issue when conflicts arose was not the legitimacy of the workers' claims to wages for work done but rather the status of their claims relative to those of others when all could not be satisfied.

During the war, military commanders and other government agents responsible for leasing plantations in occupied areas issued orders protecting the workers' right to their wages by providing, in the words of one such

17. Christian v. Crocker *et al.*, 25 Arkansas 327 (1869); Bres & O'Brien v. S. C. & J. A. Cowan, 22 Louisiana Ann. 438 (1870) (see also Lalanne Brothers v. McKinney, 28 Louisiana Ann. 642 [1876]); Huff v. Watkins, 15 South Carolina 82 (1880) (see also Richey & Miller v. DuPre, 20 South Carolina 6 [1883]); Holloway v. Brinkley, 42 Georgia 226 (1871); Smith v. Summerlin, 48 Georgia 425 (1873); Mann v. Taylor, 52 Tennessee 267 (1871). Of course, a partnership in farming could exist if that was the intent of the contracting parties. See Holfield & Company v. White, 52 Georgia 567 (1874), where the court specifically noted that the contract in this case differed from those of the 1871 and 1873 cases noted above. Here the contract indicated that the parties agreed to divide all expenses, including labor costs. Significantly in this case, neither party performed the labor; one merely agreed to provide the labor, and he hired croppers. In the earlier cases, the alleged partners were croppers. A decade later, the Georgia Supreme Court repeated its ruling that the cropper relationship did not create a partnership: Gurr v. Martin, 73 Georgia 528 (1884).

order, that "the first lien upon the crops shall be for the wages of the laborer."[18] Later, as we have seen, agents of the Freedmen's Bureau sometimes intervened when workers did not get their share by seizing crops held by merchants or planters in order to distribute them to unpaid workers. Although sparingly used and not always effective, this small protection completely disappeared with the end of wartime regulations and the departure of the bureau. Thereafter, workers had to rely upon the legislatures and the courts for guarantees that they would be paid.

Beginning in the late 1860s, each state enacted laws designed to insure that agricultural workers received their promised wages, but these laborers' lien laws, as they were called, differed significantly and had different histories.[19] Those passed by the radical legislatures provided strong legal support for the workers' claims. In Mississippi, for example, the radical legislature in 1872 gave workers a "first lien" on crops for wages due, stipulating that this lien was superior to that of "all landlords, sub-lessors, and all other persons interested in such agricultural products." Lest there be any doubts about its intent, the legislature, a year later, amended the law by explicitly extending it to those working for a share of the crop. The radicals in Arkansas and South Carolina passed similar laws specifically making the laborers' lien superior to all others including the landlord's. Georgia's 1868 Constitution provided laborers with "liens upon the property of their employers for labor performed."[20]

When the redeemers wrote or rewrote the laborers' lien laws, they subordinated the worker's lien to that of the landlord for rent and advances, allowed the landlord's lien to reach through his tenant to encumber the wages of any workers the tenant had hired, and in Mississippi and Alabama the

---

18. Article XVIII, "Rules and Regulations for Leasing Abandoned Plantations and Employing Freedmen," Memphis, Tennessee, January 7, 1864, printed in Ira Berlin *et al.* (eds.), *Freedom: A Documentary History of Emancipation, 1861–1867,* Series I, Volume III, *The Wartime Genesis of Free Labor: The Lower South* (Cambridge, 1990), 777. Similar language appeared in other orders: see Article XV, "General Orders No. 23," Headquarters, Department of the Gulf, February 3, 1864, *ibid.*, 514, and Article XV, "Adjutant General L. Thomas, Orders No. 9," Vicksburg, Mississippi, March 11, 1864, *ibid.*, 805.

19. Most states already had lien laws on the books that protected the wages of mechanics and professionals, but they did not apply to agricultural workers.

20. Mississippi, *Laws, 1872* (April 5, 1872), 131–35; Mississippi, *Laws, 1873* (April 17, 1873), 79–81; Arkansas, *Acts, 1868* (July 23, 1868), 245; South Carolina, *Acts, 1868–69* (March 19, 1869), 227–29; Article I, Section 30, Georgia 1868 Constitution.

laws specifically subordinated the laborers' liens to those of merchants who had made advances to the workers' employers.[21] These provisions in the redeemer laws seriously weakened the laborers' lien. If, as was often the case, someone rented a large tract of land and then worked it by hiring croppers, the croppers' lien for wages would not take effect until the tenant that hired them paid his rent, and if after doing so he could not pay his croppers their share, they had no recourse.[22] Similarly, if a landlord leased his land and provided supplies to his tenant who then hired wage workers or croppers, the landlord's lien for both rent and advances would be superior to the laborers' lien.[23] Finally, if a tenant hired and supplied workers himself by borrowing from a merchant, the landlord's lien for rent and usually (although there were exceptions) the merchant's lien for advances would be superior to that of the laborers.[24] In short, then, although the laborers' lien laws remained on the books, statutes and court decisions weakened their force by subordinating the worker's right to his wages to most of his employer's debts.

21. Mississippi, *Laws, 1876* (April 14, 1876), 110; Arkansas, *Acts, 1875* (January 8, 1875), 84–85, *Acts, 1883* (February 19, 1883), 32, (March 21, 1883), 176–79; Alabama, *Acts, 1874–75* (March 19, 1875), 103–106, *Acts, 1876–77* (February 9, 1877), 74–77; South Carolina, *Acts, 1877–78* (March 4, 1878), 410–11, *Acts, 1878* (December 23, 1878), 743–44, *Code of 1902*, Section 3058; Georgia, *Acts, 1873* (February 24, 1873), 42–43; Tennessee, *Acts, 1879* (January 31, 1879), 32; Texas, *General Laws, 1874* (April 4, 1874), 55–59. Louisiana is an exception. The laborers' lien law in that state was passed in March, 1867, before the radicals came to power. The law not only made "the wages of laborers" working on the crop a privileged debt on the crop produced, but "ranked [it] as the first privilege on the crop," the only one in the law that was not deemed "concurrent." Louisiana, *Acts, 1867* (March 28, 1867), 351–53. See also *Civil Code, 1870*, Sections 3217 and 3259; Moore v. Gray, 22 Louisiana Ann. 289 (1870), and Bres & O'Brien v. S. C. & J. A. Cowan, 22 Louisiana Ann. 438 (1870). In 1886, the legislature ranked existing "privileges and pledges on crops" in the following order: laborers, lessors, overseers, suppliers. *Acts, 1886* (July 8, 1886), 127.

22. Rousey v. Mattox, 111 Georgia 883, 36 S.E. 925 (1900); Hamilton v. Blanton, 107 South Carolina 142, 92 S.E. 275 (1917); Gardner v. Head, 108 Alabama 619, 18 So. 551 (1895); Land et al. v. Roby, 56 Texas C.A. 333, 120 S.W. 1057 (1909).

23. Gardner v. Head, 108 Alabama 619, 18 So. 551 (1895); Newman et al. v. Bank of Greenville et al., 66 Mississippi 323, 5 So. 753 (1889); Hollingsworth et al. v. Hill et al., 69 Mississippi 73, 10 So. 430 (1891); Burgie v. Davis, 34 Arkansas 179 (1879); Alston v. Wilson, 64 Georgia 482 (1880).

24. Sheeks-Stephen Store Co. v. Richardson, 76 Arkansas 282, 88 S.W. 983 (1905); Watson v. May, 62 Arkansas 435, 35 S.W. 1108 (1896); Birt v. Greene & Co. et al., 127 South Carolina 70, 120 S.E. 747 (1924); DuRant v. Home Bank of Barnwell, 129 South Carolina 283, 124 S.E. 12 (1924).

Weakening worker protection even further were laws that exacted heavy penalties on those who failed to complete their work or otherwise to fulfill their obligations. An 1875 Arkansas "Act to regulate the labor System" provided "that if any laborer shall, without good cause, abandon his employer prior to the expiration of his contract, he shall, thereupon, be liable to him for the full amount of any account he may owe his employer, and shall forfeit all wages due from the employer at the time of his wrongfully leaving."[25]

Other southern states imposed similar penalties on croppers who abandoned a crop. The South Carolina court ruled that "when a cropper voluntarily abandons a crop, without fault on the part of the landowner, he forfeits all interest therein."[26] The court in North Carolina came to the same conclusion, ruling in 1885 that a cropper, "having abandoned the crop in violation of his contract," could claim no rights to the crop even for the work he had already done before leaving. The Georgia lien law passed by the redeemer legislature in 1873 stated that "liens of laborers shall arise upon the completion of their contract of labor," a provision that the courts interpreted to mean that the laborer had no lien unless he could provide "evidence ... that he has fully completed his contract."[27]

A Georgia cropper discovered that strict construction of this law meant that language such as "voluntarily" abandoning a crop "without good cause" offered him scant protection when illness prevented him from completing his work. A lower court had ruled that the cropper was entitled to pay for that portion of the work he completed before becoming ill, but the supreme court reversed the decision, holding that because the cropper's failure to com-

---

25. Arkansas, *Acts, 1875* (March 6, 1875), 231. The legislature amended the 1875 act in 1883, but this provision remained unchanged in the new law. *Acts, 1883* (March 21, 1883), 178. The courts consistently upheld and enforced this provision in the law. See Hibbard v. Kirby, 38 Arkansas 102 (1881); Latham v. Barwick, 87 Arkansas 328, 113 S.W. 646 (1908); Rand v. Walton, 130 Arkansas 431, 197 S.W. 852 (1917); Crawford v. Slaten, 155 Arkansas 283, 244 S.W. 32 (1922).

26. Salley v. Cox, 94 South Carolina 216, 77 S.E. 933 (1913). This decision provoked a vigorous dissent from one justice, who argued that the cropper had grown and partially harvested the crop and therefore should receive partial payment for work done, but a later decision sustained the majority, specifically noting that when a cropper abandoned a crop he breached his contract for hire "which barred a recovery upon a quantum meruit," *i.e.*, to receive as much as he deserves. Hardwick v. Page, 124 South Carolina 111, 117 S.E. 204 (1923).

27. Thigpen v. Leigh, 93 North Carolina 47 (1885); Georgia, *Acts, 1873* (February 24, 1873), 43; Harvey v. Lewis, 19 Georgia App. 655, 91 S.E. 1052 (1917) and earlier cases cited therein.

plete his work "was due to his own misfortune in being unable to work, as a result of sickness, and not to any act of the landlord," he therefore lost his laborer's lien rights.[28]

Should an employer have cause to discharge a cropper, the worker would suffer the same penalties. Thus, when a Georgia landowner discharged a cropper for taking for his own use some of the crop he was growing, the court ruled that this was adequate cause for discharge and that as a result the cropper lost his right to a laborer's lien because he failed to complete his contract.[29]

Laws that imposed such heavy penalties on croppers who left their work or were discharged gave employers a powerful weapon of control over their labor force, including opportunities for unscrupulous employers to defraud their croppers. Bettie Lewis, a Georgia cropper, seems to have been the victim of such an attempt. She contracted to work "a one-horse farm" for one Henry Owens, who had rented the land on which she was to work. She had "made the crop and had almost harvested it" when the landowner allegedly began foreclosure proceedings against Owens. The sheriff seized that portion of the crop already harvested; he then hired Lewis to harvest what remained, then seized that as well and refused to pay Lewis. Ordinarily, this would probably have ended the matter for a cropper too poor to hire a lawyer, but Lewis apparently received help, for she sought court action to get her share under the laborer's lien law. The judge of the City Court of Saudersville dismissed Lewis' claim on the grounds that she had not completed the labor as specified in the contract, blithely ignoring the fact that the sheriff's intervention had prevented her from completing the work under the terms of the original agreement. Apparently, Lewis continued to receive support, for she was able to take an appeal to the supreme court, which unanimously reversed the lower court's decision without feeling the need to justify its decision beyond setting out the facts of the case. Under Georgia law, the landowner did have a right to the cropper's share if Owens was really his tenant and if the cropper's share was needed to pay the

28. Gardner v. Smith, 39 Georgia App. 224 (1929).
29. Payne v. Trammell, 29 Georgia App. 475, 115 S.E. 923 (1923). Contracts with tenants could also be broken for the same reason. In Louisiana, if tenants gave inadequate attention to their work the landlord could stop advances, repossess any of his property, and take over the crops: Harrison v. Goldberg, 133 Louisiana 389, 63 So. 59 (1913); Dixon v. Alford, 143 So. 679 (Louisiana App. 1932); Dixon v. Watson, 143 So. 683 (Louisiana App. 1932).

rent. The failure of the landowner to join the suit and the silence of the court on the landlord's rights suggest that the whole proceeding was simply a fraudulent attempt by Owens to deprive the cropper of her wages.[30]

Lewis' successful case indicated that even the weakened laborers' lien laws could offer workers some limited protection if they were enforced fairly and equitably. Outright fraud, of course, was illegal but difficult to prove, requiring evidence of deliberate misrepresentation or deceit. In any event, croppers who believed they had been fraudulently deprived of their wages had to persuade local authorities to undertake prosecution of offending landowners. Otherwise, croppers had to take the initiative and institute civil proceedings to enforce their laborer's lien. In such instances, the social context as well as the nature of the law itself gave the landowner-employer a clear advantage.

The landowner-cropper relationship was ostensibly even-handed and equitable, a contract between employer and employee entailing legal responsibilities and obligations on both sides. But because the law put ownership and control of the crop in the hands of the landowner, if he failed to pay his croppers their wages, dismissed them without adequate cause, or otherwise failed to fulfill his obligations, he nevertheless retained legal ownership of the entire crop. Croppers who remained unpaid had to begin civil proceedings under the laborers' lien laws or for breach of contract to get the courts to order the employer to pay their wages. This entailed legal expenses that few could afford. Wealthy landowners, on the other hand, could afford good lawyers and had the added advantage of sympathetic judges and juries, especially if the cropper were black. If a judgment went against the cropper, he had the right to appeal to higher courts, requiring additional costs that in all likelihood would exceed the amount claimed. As a result, few cases involving the laborers' lien laws reached the courts. Those such as Lewis' that did must have had the sympathetic support of wealthy and influential people in the area who found the behavior of a landowner to be especially unfair.

This is clearly revealed in another Georgia case that involved particularly egregious behavior by a landowner which, the evidence clearly revealed, won the cropper the sympathy of the local white population. The case began in 1921 when Lee Bussell, an Irwin County landowner, attempted to deprive his black cropper, Colonel Bishop, of his wages by driving him from

30. Lewis v. Owens, 124 Georgia 228, 52 S.E. 333 (1905).

the land and then taking his entire crop on grounds that the cropper had abandoned it. When threats failed to get Bishop to leave, Bussell, along with some of his friends, beat and then shot the cropper. This upset some whites in the neighborhood who assisted Bishop in getting a court injunction prohibiting Bussell from forcing Bishop to abandon the crop. They told the local court that, although Bishop was "old, one-armed, and suffering under the serious disability of wounds caused by the shots and licks inflicted upon him by . . . [Bussell] and his confederates," he had a large family that would help him gather the crops. A number of "reputable white men" agreed to oversee the harvest and a settlement with Bussell. The court granted the injunction and appointed a receiver to supervise the gathering of the crop.

The landowner, however, stubbornly persisted; although he would receive his legitimate portion of the crop under this court-ordered arrangement, he appealed to a higher court to vacate the injunction, insisting that he had a right to dismiss the cropper. In its decision, the supreme court carefully outlined the law so as not to establish the wrong precedent. It agreed that because Bishop was a cropper, he was a mere employee; therefore his employer had the right to discharge him. If discharged, the cropper had to leave, although he could later bring a civil suit for "breach of contract" against his former employer for any wages due him for work done before his discharge if he could prove that he had been wrongfully discharged. Ordinarily, therefore, an injunction preventing an employer from discharging his cropper would be improper. But this was a special case, the court continued, because the landowner had not simply dismissed his cropper but had used violence in an attempt to force the cropper "to break his contract and to abandon his crop." Therefore, the court ruled, the injunction was proper under these special circumstances.[31]

Although if given the opportunity the courts sometimes protected croppers such as Bettie Lewis and Colonel Bishop who were victims of gross mistreatment,[32] usually they were not so sympathetic, as an Arkansas cropper

---

31. Bussell v. Bishop, 152 Georgia 428, 110 S.E. 174 (1921). Testimony in the case revealed that Bussell had employed Bishop during the two previous years and had paid him nothing.

32. For a case in Texas similar to that of Bussell v. Bishop, see Barnett v. Govan, 241 S.W. 276 (Texas C.A., 1922). When a cropper in Hertford County, North Carolina, died before completing the harvest, his landlord tried to take the entire crop, claiming that by dying the cropper had abandoned it. The court refused to accept this and awarded the crop-

discovered. When he resisted his landowner's efforts to get him to abandon his crop and thereby lose any wages due, the landowner tore down and removed the house in which he was living, making it impossible for him to remain at work. The cropper sought legal redress, but the court ruled against him on the grounds that he had no right to the house, adding that only if the cropper could prove in a separate court action that he had been wrongfully discharged could he collect damages.[33]

When evidence of blatant fraud or gross inequities led the higher courts to rule against landowners, they carefully avoided setting any precedents that might strengthen the laborers' lien laws. Thus in a Georgia case involving a cropper who left before completing the harvest, the court ruled that his employer had legally seized the entire crop and denied the cropper any portion of it. The court was unmoved by the cropper's argument that he had to leave in order to earn enough to feed himself because his employer would not provide him food and refused to pay him his share of the produce already harvested. The laborers' lien did not have force until the cropper fulfilled the terms of his contract, the court ruled in dismissing the cropper's claim. The court cited ample precedent to support its decision and specifically noted that its decision in the earlier case involving the cropper Bettie Lewis was not relevant because in that instance the cropper was physically and unlawfully prevented from completing her work.[34]

Should a cropper manage to bring a civil suit and prove that he had been wrongfully ejected, the courts were very protective of the landowners' interests when assessing how much the ejected cropper could claim. An Arkansas court, for example, ruled that the laborer wrongfully expelled could collect damages to the extent of what "he would have earned for his services under the contract if he had been permitted to perform the contract, less what he earned in other employment or could by reasonable effort have earned during the unexpired period." Other state courts ruled in much the same way.[35]

Criminal law gave employers additional protection along with addi-

---

per's heirs his share less the cost of completing the harvest. Parker v. Brown, 136 North Carolina 280, 48 S.E. 657 (1904).

33. Woodson *et ux.* v. McLaughlin *et al.*, 150 Arkansas 340, 234 S.W. 185 (1921).

34. Harvey v. Lewis, 19 Georgia App. 655, 91 S.E. 1052 (1917).

35. Somers v. Musolf, 86 Arkansas 97, 109 S.W. 1173 (1908). The Texas courts, however, provided wrongfully evicted croppers with a bit more protection. If the cropper were

tional control over their croppers. Because the crop belonged to the landowner until he divided it—that is, until he paid his workers their wages—a cropper could be charged with theft if he removed or sold any part of it before the division was made, including that part that eventually—that is, after the division—would in fact be his. In 1898 in Abbeville County, South Carolina, Isaac Saunders was convicted of grand larceny for selling a portion of the crop on which he had been working. In his appeal, Saunders argued that his contract to work for a portion of the crop made him a partner of his landlord, and this gave him the right to sell his portion of the crop whenever he chose to do so. The supreme court upheld the conviction, ruling that Saunders was a cropper, which made him a worker (the court used the term *servant*), not a partner, and as such "is not the owner of the crop, and no specific crop, or specific part thereof, is vested" in him.[36]

wrongfully evicted after the crops had fully matured, he could collect his full share, but if evicted earlier, the deductions indicated were appropriate. Relevant cases are Tignor v. Toney, 13 Texas C.A. 518, 35 S.W. 881 (1896), and Fagan v. Vogt, 35 Texas C.A. 528, 80 S.W. 664 (1904), in which the court ruled that the cropper was to receive a full share; and Rogers v. McGuffey, 96 Texas 565, 74 S.W. 753 (1903), and Matthews v. Foster, 238 S.W. 317 (Texas C.A., 1922), that applied the contrary ruling. The court explained the law and its various applications in Crews v. Cortez, 102 Texas 111, 113 S.W. 523 (1908). Tenants, of course, could not claim rights under the laborers' lien law, but if unlawfully forced from the land they too could recover their interest in the crop. A Texas court ruled that "the amount of damages sustained by . . . [the ousted tenant] would be the reasonable market value of his part of the crops which it was reasonably probable he would have raised on the farm during the year, less the expense of raising and harvesting them, and less such sums of money as . . . [he] and the dependent members of his family could have earned during the same year by engaging in other business": Rupert v. Swindle, 212 S.W. 670 (Texas C.A., 1919). In a Louisiana case, the evidence showed that the landowner had forced his tenant to leave the land after the crop had been grown but before it had been harvested. The landlord then gathered the crop and sold it. The court ruled that because the tenant had been wrongfully discharged, he had a right to his share of the crop: Young v. Gay, 41 Louisiana Ann. 758, 6 So. 608 (1889). In order to retain their shares, tenants had to convince the court that they had been wrongfully discharged. Evidence in two cases cited above (note 29), which reached the Louisiana Appeals Court in 1932, revealed that a landlord had stopped advances promised to two tenants and taken the crops of both, claiming that the tenants had neglected their work to the detriment of the landlord's interests. The court ruled that in one case the evidence proved the landlord to be correct and awarded him the tenant's crop: Dixon v. Alford, 143 So. 679 (Louisiana App. 1932). But in the other case, the court decided that the evidence showed that the landlord improperly took the crop and ordered the tenant's share (less expenses) returned to him: Dixon v. Watson, 143 So. 683 (Louisiana App. 1932).

36. State v. Saunders, 52 South Carolina 580, 30 S.E. 616 (1898).

Twenty years later, in a similar case, the South Carolina high court upheld both the grand larceny conviction of two Lee County croppers who had sold the crop on which they had been working and the conviction of the buyer for receiving stolen merchandise. The cropper "had no right, title, or interest" in the crop until his landlord divided it and gave him his share, repeated the court in its ruling. Similarly, a North Carolina court ruled that a cropper who fed a portion of the crop he had grown to his stock was properly indicted for theft.[37]

Like any other property owner, landlords had the right to use force if necessary to protect their property, which meant that before the division they had the right to use force to prevent a cropper from taking any portion of the crop, including the portion that eventually would be his share. Justifiable force even included homicide, announced a Virginia court in a case involving a dispute between a landowner and his cropper over the disposition of thirty-one bushels of corn and $18 worth of tobacco produced by the cropper. The landlord locked the crops in his shed, and when the cropper attempted to break in and remove them, the landlord killed him. A Goochland County court convicted the landlord of second-degree murder, but the state supreme court overruled the lower court, declaring that the crop until divided belonged to the landowner, and he had a right to defend his property from anyone trying to steal it.[38]

The protection of the criminal law did not extend to workers, however. Because the landowner owned the entire crop until he divided it with his croppers, he could not be indicted for embezzlement or theft, even if he took the entire crop and refused to pay his workers. The only redress available to the unpaid workers and to any of their creditors was civil action under the laborers' lien laws or for breach of contract. When a North Carolina landowner was convicted of embezzlement for selling the entire crop grown on his land and not paying his cropper, the supreme court overturned the conviction, arguing that the landowner's action was merely "a breach of trust .... No statute has made it a crime." When an Oklahoma landlord prevented a cropper from completing work on a crop and refused to pay him for work done, the court ruled that the landlord could not be accused of "conversion"

37. State v. Sanders *et al.*, 110 South Carolina 487, 96 S.E. 622 (1918); Varner v. Spencer *et al.*, 72 North Carolina 381 (1875).

38. State v. Austin, 123 North Carolina 749, 31 S.E. 731 (1898); Parrish v. The Commonwealth, 81 Virginia 1 (1884).

(illegally taking the property of another); because the crop, until divided, belonged to the employer, the landlord could be guilty of nothing more than a breach of contract—a civil, not a criminal, offense. The South Carolina high court refused to allow the creation of a contrary precedent even when its ruling might constitute a "hardship," as it did in a case in 1915. A landlord in Dillion County released his interest in his croppers' shares, whereupon a merchant provided the croppers with supplies. When, after the harvest, the landlord took the entire crop, the merchant sued to have him indicted for appropriating his property. The court, admitting that there might be "a hardship in this case," nevertheless ruled that the landlord could not be indicted because until a division was made he owned the entire crop even though he had agreed to release his interest in the croppers' shares.[39]

In sum, the landlord-cropper relationship provided landlords with the legal protection of employers, allowing them to direct the work of the croppers and giving them ownership and control of the product, subject to the payment of wages due. Landlords also found additional ways to control their work force, ways that often extended their control beyond working hours.

Because croppers were not paid until the end of the crop year and ordinarily owned little property, they invariably needed advances on their wages for food, clothing, and other goods and services they might need during the year. Landowner-employers quickly realized that their ability to control these advances, which directly affected the well-being of the croppers and their families, could be a powerful weapon to insure their croppers' obedience—unless, of course, the cropper could get advances from other sources. A landlord seeking to close off other sources of advances might require that his croppers (as well as his wage hands and tenants) trade with his plantation store or with a particular merchant of his choosing.

During the early postbellum years landlords found this a difficult requirement to enforce, or more precisely they found it a dangerous requirement to enforce, because many merchants would also supply the credit sought, and the early lien laws seemed to protect the merchants at the expense of landlords. Although the revised crop lien laws gave precedence to landlords who advanced supplies, the laws did not *require* that workers and tenants

---

39. State v. Keith, 126 North Carolina 1114, 36 S.E. 169 (1900); Taylor v. Higgins, 129 Oklahoma 57, 263 P. 146 (1928); Malcolm Mercantile Co. v. Britt, 102 South Carolina 499, 87 S.E. 143 (1915).

borrow from their landlords. The landlords, like some other nineteenth-century employers, quickly discovered, however, that if they paid their workers in scrip redeemable only in a store of the landlords' choosing, usually the plantation store, they could achieve the desired control — and get by with less ready cash to boot.

In response to complaints about this practice, the radical legislature in South Carolina in 1872 enacted a law requiring anyone employing "laborers on plantations or elsewhere" to pay wages in United States currency and punishing by fine and/or imprisonment any employer paying in "scrip of any description." When planters continued to issue scrip, maintaining that these were advances, not wages, the radical legislature responded in 1875 by making this practice illegal as well. Once the redeemers gained control of the legislature, they began to remove these restrictions. An 1879 amendment allowed employers to pay any advances in scrip or orders on plantation stores, although final settlement had to be in cash. But even this little protection for agricultural workers completely disappeared in 1901 when a new law that continued to restrict the use of scrip to pay wages, concluded with the statement that its "provisions . . . shall not apply to agricultural contracts or advances made for agricultural purposes."[40]

Although scrip redeemable only in plantation stores continued to be used, changes in the lien laws effectively achieved the same results. As we have seen, a tenant's lien to a merchant was always subordinate to the lien of his landlord for both rent and advances, making it very risky to lend to tenants unless the landlord waived his rights. But for anyone other than his employer, lending to a cropper could be even more risky. Because a cropper might receive advances on his wages from his employer, the amount of which did not have to be recorded publicly, a lender could have no idea how much, if anything, a cropper would eventually receive and therefore had no idea how much he could safely lend. Although, as the Georgia court ruled, the cropper had a "mortgageable interest" in the crop that "may ripen into a title" once debts to the landlord were paid, the problem for potential lenders to croppers was that they had no way to be certain that this "mortgageable interest" would in fact ever "ripen into a title."[41]

40. South Carolina, *Acts, 1871–72* (March 13, 1872), 216; South Carolina, *Acts, 1874–75* (March 11, 1875), 999 (The new law also increased the maximum fines and imprisonment); South Carolina, *Acts, 1879–80* (December 12, 1879), 7; South Carolina, *Acts 1901* (February 20, 1901), 746–47; *Civil Code, 1902,* Section 2719.

41. Fountain v. Fountain, 10 Georgia App. 758, 73 S.E. 1096 (1912).

A dispute in North Carolina illustrated the dangers a merchant might encounter even when he executed a lien on a cropper's wages. Two croppers signed a written agreement with a merchant in which they promised to pay for goods advanced out of their share of a crop. At the end of the year, the landlord took the entire crop, sold it, and appropriated all the proceeds. He refused to honor the merchant's claim, arguing that the advances he had made to the croppers completely absorbed their share. The merchant sued, insisting that his contract preceded that of the advances made by the landlord. The court sided with the landlord. The croppers, it ruled, were to be paid "one half of the crop, or of its value, as wages," subject to the advances the landlord had provided. The croppers "had interests which they could and did assign" to the merchant, "but the value of those interests could be ascertained only after deducting the lawful charges of . . . [the landlord]; and it seems that after this deduction nothing is left." The croppers had a lien for their wages, but these wages had been paid in the form of the landlord's advances, "so that nothing is due" the merchant.[42]

In a decision a decade later, the North Carolina court ruled that even when a surplus remained, a lender might be unable to claim it. The dispute involved a cropper who had abandoned the crop. After the landlord completed work on the crop, took his share, and deducted all of his expenses, he still had a balance but nonetheless refused to pay a merchant who claimed he had a lien for an advance given the departed cropper. The court ruled that the landlord had no obligation to pay the merchant, declaring that when the cropper abandoned the crop, his "right to a share of the crop . . . ceased," and therefore the merchant's "lien on the share necessarily ceased with it."[43]

In the course of this ruling, the North Carolina court seemed to raise questions about the ability of a cropper to give a lien on the crop. A lien, it explained, "is simply the right to have a demand satisfied out of the property of another," but a cropper did not own the crop on which he worked until his employer paid him his share. Rulings in other states similarly suggested that the cropper's legal status as a worker made it doubtful that he could give a crop lien at all. A cropper "could not execute a mortgage which would operate as a lien upon property he did not own," ruled a Texas court in 1872, and he would not own any of the crop until his employer paid him his portion after first deducting any advances he had provided. The

42. Hudgins v. Wood, 72 North Carolina 256 (1875).
43. Thigpen v. Leigh, 93 North Carolina 47 (1885).

Georgia court that same year came to the same conclusion: "no person can purchase or take a lien on the wages of the cropper, to-wit: his share of the crop until the bargain be completed." In a landowner-cropper relationship, ruled the Arkansas court, the crop belongs to the landowner, and the cropper "had no interest in it he could sell or mortgage." The court in South Carolina ruled flatly that a cropper could not give a lien on the crop he would produce because he did not own the crop and had only a claim for wages.[44]

In sum, then, although a cropper might give a lien or a mortgage on what he eventually would get, uncertainties over what, if anything, he would actually receive made lending to croppers risky unless the lender received some sort of guarantee from the landlord. Cases continued to arise not because lenders were ignorant of the law and the risks entailed, but rather because they had taken liens thinking that their borrowers were tenants, not croppers.

Some landlords sought to extend their control over their work force and to maintain its stability by restricting the right of workers to leave their employ. The laws depriving croppers and tenants who left in the middle of the season of any rights to the crop probably kept some at work even when other opportunities might be available. But for workers who had already received advances that promised to absorb much of what they would earn, abandoning a growing crop might not entail significant loss if they could find work elsewhere. A successful landlord suit for breach of contract would mean little, because even if the worker were found, he would surely be without resources. Attempts to forge agreements among employers to refrain from hiring each other's workers proved difficult to sustain even among neighbors and impossible to achieve at a distance.

When informal agreements failed, landlords turned to the legislatures for help, but the resulting legislation proved ineffective. The so-called anti-enticement laws made it a criminal offense to hire a worker already under contract, but the courts were reluctant to impose criminal penalties on influential planters, who of course would be the main offenders, and it proved difficult to prove that a planter knowingly employed a worker already under contract.[45] The courts in some states found the laws to be unconstitu-

44. McGee v. Fitzer, 37 Texas 27 (1872–73); Appling v. Odom and Mercier, 46 Georgia 583 (1872); Ponder v. Rhea, 32 Arkansas 435 (1877); Carpenter v. Strickland, 20 South Carolina 1 (1883); Richey & Miller v. DuPre, 20 South Carolina 6 (1883).

45. Alabama enacted its anti-enticement law in 1866. Anyone who "knowingly" hired a worker under contract could be convicted of a misdemeanor. The offending enticer had

tional because they infringed on the right to contract and imposed criminal penalties for a civil offense.[46]

Even if strictly enforced, however, the anti-enticement laws could not prevent the hiring of workers for a new season after their contracts for the current year had expired. Laws restricting the activities of labor recruiters or requiring that they purchase expensive licenses hindered but did not stop their work.[47] Furthermore, the regular movement of many tenants and croppers at the end of every crop season clearly indicated that workers seeking to move did not need the recruiters to tell them where to go.

Several state legislatures, seeking to avoid placing criminal sanctions on landlords while still allowing them to restrict the movement of their croppers and tenants, enacted legislation aimed solely at the offending workers

---

to be found and presented with evidence that the worker he had hired was in fact under contract to another. If he then refused to release the worker he could be charged but had to be convicted by a jury. Alabama, *Acts, 1866* (February 16, 1866), 111–12. Georgia's courts construed its anti-enticement acts (Georgia, *Acts, 1901* [December 17, 1901], 63, *Acts, 1903* [August 7, 1903], 91, *Civil Code, 1910*, Sections 3712 and 3713) very strictly, giving the enticer every benefit of doubt. See, for example, Polk v. Thomason, 130 Georgia 542, 61 S.E. 123 (1908), and Steward v. Hill et al., 134 Georgia 596, 68 S.E. 328 (1910), in which the state supreme court sustained an acquittal and overthrew a conviction. South Carolina passed its anti-enticement law in 1880; anyone found guilty could be fined and imprisoned. South Carolina, *Acts, 1880* (December 24, 1880), 423. An Arkansas law of 1875 allowed an employer to sue an enticer for damages: Arkansas, *Acts, 1875* (March 6, 1875), 230–32. An 1883 amendment added criminal penalties and increased liabilities. Anyone convicted of enticing a worker under contract could be fined and was liable for double damages: Arkansas, *Acts, 1883* (March 21, 1883), 176–79. Under Mississippi's 1890 anti-enticement law, anyone found guilty of employing a worker or tenant under contract would be fined and was liable for double the damages sustained by the worker's employer: Mississippi, *Acts, 1890* (February 21, 1890), 69; Mississippi, *Code, 1892*, Section 1068. In 1900 the legislature amended the law, dropping the provision for double damages; only damages actually incurred could be collected: Mississippi, *Acts, 1900* (March 12, 1900), 140.

46. The Georgia Supreme Court declared the law unconstitutional in 1913, ruling it "arbitrary" and an "unreasonable restriction on the right to contract": Fortune v. Braswell, 139 Georgia 609, 77 S.E. 818 (1913). The court's major concern was for the employer; it refused to consider "the question as to whether the practical working of the act may produce a state of peonage." In Alabama the high court ruled that the 1901 law penalizing workers who left before the expiration of their contracts was an unconstitutional infringement on the right to contract: Toney v. State, 141 Alabama 120 (1904).

47. Alabama, for example, required "emigrant agents" seeking to hire laborers to work in another state to pay $500 for an annual license. Recruiters failing to do so could be fined and jailed at hard labor. Alabama, *Acts, 1903* (October 1, 1903), 344–45.

rather than at those who hired them. Laws in South Carolina, Georgia, and Alabama declared that anyone who took an advance and then failed to fulfill his contract could be convicted of fraud. Such laws in effect made the breaking of contractual obligations a criminal as well as a civil offense, and they therefore allowed the police to return the offending worker and the courts to punish him by fines and imprisonment. In practice, the landlords would often pay the fines, add the cost to the worker's advance, and put him back to work. Despite their manifest unconstitutionality—they permitted imprisonment for debt and peonage, a form of involuntary servitude—some of these laws remained in force well into the twentieth century.[48]

These attempts to restrict worker mobility, although obviously manifesting cruelty and unfairness, did not become a central feature in the labor market because landowners found that they could get the labor they needed without such restrictive laws. Each year thousands of tenants and croppers moved from one place to another seeking better conditions, but for the landowners the movement amounted to little more than labor turnover, inconvenient, perhaps, but not causing a dangerous shortage of needed workers.

48. South Carolina, *Acts, 1897* (March 2, 1897), 457. Georgia, *Acts, 1903* (August 15, 1903), 90; Alabama, *Code, 1896,* Section 4730; Alabama, *Acts, 1903* (October 1, 1903), 345–46, *Acts, 1907* (August 15, 1907), 636–37. The Alabama Supreme Court repeatedly found the state's law to be constitutional, ruling that the law did not punish the failure to pay a debt but rather the "fraudulent practices" of taking money without the intention of fulfilling the obligations for which the money was paid. See Bailey v. State, 158 Alabama 18, 48 So. 498 (1908), and the cases cited therein. The U.S. Supreme Court was not impressed by such reasoning and declared the law unconstitutional in Bailey v. Alabama, 219 U.S. 219 (1911). The Alabama legislature promptly reenacted essentially the same law with a few minor changes ostensibly designed to remedy the problems identified by the Supreme Court: Alabama, *General Laws, 1911* (March 9, 1911), 93–94. The Georgia Supreme Court ruled the Georgia law to be constitutional (Lamar v. State, 120 Georgia 312, 47 S.E. 958 [1904]; Townsend v. State, 124 Georgia 69, 52 S.E. 293 [1905]), a view it continued to hold even after the Bailey decision in the U.S. Supreme Court in 1911 (Wilson v. State, 138 Georgia 489, 75 S.E. 619 [1912]). The Georgia law remained in force until 1942, when the U.S. Supreme Court declared it unconstitutional: Taylor v. Georgia, 315 U.S. 25 (1942). On these and similar laws, see Oscar Zeichner, "The Legal Status of the Agricultural Laborer in the South," *Political Science Quarterly,* LV (September, 1940), 424–28; Pete Daniel, *The Shadow of Slavery: Peonage in the South, 1901–1969* (Urbana, 1972); William Cohen, "Negro Involuntary Servitude in the South, 1865–1940: A Preliminary Analysis," *Journal of Southern History,* XLII (February, 1976), 31–60; William Cohen, *At Freedom's Edge: Black Mobility and the Southern Quest for Racial Control, 1861–1915* (Baton Rouge, 1991), 228–47 and *passim.*

The protection of the freedmen that the Freedmen's Bureau and the radical legislatures had forced on unwilling planters was meager and limited at best. The bureau advocated the written contract spelling out the obligations and the rights of employer and employee as a means to discipline the freedmen and the planters to a new and unfamiliar free labor system by providing employers with a labor force and employees with guarantees of a fair return for their efforts. Within a generation the contract, increasingly vague and usually oral, primarily protected the employers, its guarantees for the worker sharply limited and subordinated to those of the landlord. Share wages, which many workers thought would give them a direct stake in their work, perhaps as partners but certainly with some management prerogatives, became merely a form of wage labor in which wages were paid in kind. Croppers not only had no voice in farm management, but many also found the rigorous discipline of the workplace extended into their nonworking hours. Most tenants were hardly better off. If traditional tenancy law gave tenants control over their output and management rights, the legislatures and the courts gradually altered the law to make it possible for those planters who desired to do so to exercise as much control over tenants as they did over croppers and money-wage workers. When landlords, content merely to collect their rents, failed to impose these restrictions on the tenants, merchants from whom most tenants borrowed did so. Small landowners, when they turned to merchants for advances, as most did, also lost much of their management independence and increasingly lost their lands as well.

It would seem that the most obvious conclusion to draw is that the crop lien laws and the laws concerning landlord-tenant and landlord-cropper relations created a repressive labor system that gave property-owning landlords almost complete control of their workforce and gave merchants, who through foreclosures and purchases increasingly became landowners themselves, much the same control over the tenants and the small farmers with whom they dealt. Some historians have argued that tenancy and the crop lien laws created a postbellum system that was little more than slavery with a new name. Indeed, as the farmers' alliances charged, the new system was even more pernicious than the old for it enthralled not only the blacks but a majority of the white farmers as well.

Repressive as the new system was, however, it would be misleading to see it as little more than a continuation of slavery under a new guise. If the legal changes supported a clearly repressive society that fell far short of what the freedmen and their northern and southern supporters had envisioned following emancipation, they did nevertheless support a free labor system in the postwar South, a system that in its essential features replicated that of the North.

CHAPTER FOUR

"The Important Business of Farming with Hired Labor"
Law and Postbellum Southern Society

The law—legislation and the rulings of courts and government regulatory agencies—significantly affects both our public and our private lives. Civil rights, voting, and tax laws; court rulings on school segregation, abortion, and the rights of those accused of a crime; and rules set down by OSHA, the SEC, the IRS, and the Federal Reserve Board—just to mention a few examples—illustrate how profoundly the law can promote and direct important social, political, and economic change. Yet the law is profoundly conservative in its procedures and practices, and in the underlying ideological assumptions governing these procedures and practices.

By establishing the "rules of the game," that is, what is acceptable behavior and what is not, the law seeks to conserve or maintain proper norms of behavior by providing sanctions against those who depart from such norms and by providing the means to decide what those proper norms are when disagreements arise. The procedure used in resolving differences reinforces the conservatism of the law. Litigation before the courts involves disputes over one or both of two issues—what actually took place and, given such events, what is the appropriate law governing such events that will resolve the disputes. When a jury is involved, its task is to determine what happened when there is some doubt, that is, when the litigants disagree about what happened.[1] But the judge, not the jury, determines the law appropriate to the case; the jury only decides the facts.

---

1. A jury trial may be waived if both parties agree on the facts or agree to allow the judge to decide based upon evidence presented to him.

The jury hears the conflicting evidence from both sides in a dispute, but the judge intervenes in the jury's deliberations in two ways, both based upon what he determines to be the appropriate law. First, the judge decides what evidence lawyers on each side may present to the jury, basing his decision on the admissibility of the evidence given the law concerning the issues at hand. Second, when all the admissible evidence has been presented, the judge then instructs the jury, informing it of the applicable law, thereby setting boundaries within which the jury must decide.[2] Should there be an appeal to a higher court, the appellant ordinarily cannot question the jury's decision.[3] Instead he must question the court's reading of the law, which usually involves evidence the judge allowed to be presented and/or the kind of instructions the judge gave to the jury. In either case, the issue would be what the law was. If the judge in a lower court misread the existing law and thereby deprived the appellant of his rights, the higher court will reverse the decision of the lower and either allow its decision to replace that of the lower court or, more commonly, order that the case be retried below. But if it decides that the judge in the lower court was correct in his reading of the law, the appellate court will allow the decision to stand.

In theory, then, the judge does not make the law; this is the task of the legislature. The judge merely determines the applicable law governing the particular circumstances and then applies it. In practice, of course, the distinction between making and finding existing law is more easily stated as a principle than applied. Because legislation cannot cover in detail every possible conflict that may arise under its provisions, if only because changing conditions create unforeseen results, the court must determine in the particular case before it what the law is when existing legislation is silent or ambiguous concerning the exact issues arising in the dispute.

In doing so, judges (and the attorneys on both sides in a dispute) rely

---

2. If he believes it warranted, the judge may give a "peremptory instruction" to the jury instructing it that it *must* return a verdict for one or the other party in the dispute. A judge may also stop the case from going to a jury and order a "directed verdict" if he decides that the evidence presented does not warrant the jury's consideration because under the law only one decision is possible.

3. An exception, of course, would be if the appellant could prove that the jury was in some way tainted by including members who had a vested interest in the outcome of the case or who had been bribed or intimidated by parties in the case. For example, in recent years, civil rights advocates have successfully challenged jury decisions because of the systematic exclusion of blacks or other minorities from juries.

upon two methods. They look back to the legislation in an effort to determine the intent of the legislatures that passed the laws, and they look to precedents, that is, to the ways in which other courts have ruled in similar cases. Both methods are conservative in that both are based upon the notion that the laws—the rules of the game—are set and that the task of the court is to find the appropriate applicable law(s) in the case before it. And both methods preserve the theory that judges merely apply the law and do not make it. Because in most instances both sides in a dispute accept the courts' rulings concerning what the law is after all avenues of appeal have been exhausted, the conservatism and the theory remain untouched.

The acceptance of the procedure does not mean that everyone is satisfied with the law and the results it produces—at least, in the results produced by the way in which a court rules. Those dissatisfied may use the appeal process to persuade a higher court to reverse a lower court that allegedly misunderstood or misread the law. Although the U.S. Supreme Court is the court of last appeal, even a decision by that court does not necessarily end matters. Ordinarily, but not inevitably, the court will not depart from established precedents—the doctrine of *stare decisis*—but a new law that meets the court's objections or another, better-argued case might lead to a different decision.

The process I have described supports the traditional values of the American political system—the separation of powers and its underlying democratic intent (the elected representatives of the people make the law and the judges merely apply it when disputes arise), and equality of all before the law (the law established by the people's representatives applies to all regardless of station). This process also creates and perpetuates the notion that the law is somehow above politics, independent of the political struggles that engulf the legislatures. All federal judges are appointed for life, as are some state judges, the others ordinarily appointed for long terms. This is supposed to insulate judges from politics. Even judges who are elected usually serve long terms, and they too are supposed to be above politics, their election campaigns stressing that they are better qualified and more experienced in knowing and applying the law than their opponents. The education of lawyers perpetuates this same view of the law. Law schools teach students how to discover what the law is in particular situations so as to be able to advise their clients and, should litigation occur, to present the evidence necessary to support their clients' interests by convincing judges that their reading of the law is correct. In sum, therefore, resolution of legal disputes simply requires ascertaining the relevant facts and then discovering and applying the appropriate, existing law, a process that is ostensibly both apolitical and fair so long as lawyers and judges are honest and competent.

If the law is supposed to be above politics, it nevertheless is a form of social control that makes it profoundly political. By setting down certain rules of behavior and providing a means to settle differences, the law reflects both the norms and the goals of a society as enunciated by the legislatures and then applied by the courts and, increasingly in recent years, by administrative agencies. The most obvious ways in which the law acts as a form of social control are in its coercive features, in the criminal law, which prohibits certain kinds of behavior and imposes sanctions on those who are convicted of such behavior, and in the civil law—commercial law, contract law, and torts—which defines legal behavior and provides redress for those who can prove they have been wronged.

Law not only imposes sanctions on those who do not play by the rules of the game, it also provides an ideological form of social control. It influences how people behave, not simply because they fear the sanctions, but because they come to accept the rules as the only proper way to act. This ideological hegemony does not mean that everyone obeys the law; some do not follow the rules of the game and, if caught, are brought before the court which determines whether they are guilty and must suffer the sanctions the law imposes. But most legal conflicts, especially those concerning civil law, do not arise from deliberate, willful disobedience. Some think they are following the rules, but those with whom they deal disagree, and the courts are called upon to resolve the disagreement by determining which rules apply in the dispute. Others initiate legal conflict by challenging a particular law as contradicting a higher or superior law as, for example, when state laws are said to contradict state constitutions, federal laws, or the federal constitution. In such cases, the courts must resolve the alleged contradiction.

The very *process* by which the rules are enforced reinforces the ideological function of the law—the acceptance of the notion that there are proper rules of behavior that all must follow, that those who do not deserve to be punished, and that when there is disagreement over what is proper behavior lawyers and judges, by examining constitutions, legislation, and past decisions, can discover those rules and apply them fairly and impartially. This notion, of course, is part of a long tradition in the United States. We have "a government of laws, not of men," wrote John Adams in 1779, and his words have been regularly repeated ever since.

If Americans believe that the law is somehow removed from social, political, economic, and ideological conflicts, at the same time they have always seen the law as an important means to solve problems and to direct, facilitate, and/or control social, economic and political change. Americans expect politicians to respond to demands for legal changes deemed necessary to correct inequities and to solve problems, and these demands usually elicit hot political debate over what new laws are necessary and proper. Significantly, however, the relationship between law and politics remains obscure even in the midst of such debates because they usually are clothed in conservative legal terms. New laws are needed to solve new problems arising from changed conditions that allow the intent of the existing law to be perverted. Loopholes that permit actions unanticipated by the laws' authors must be closed; local laws that go counter to national laws must be amended or repealed; and all laws that go counter to constitutional guarantees must be changed.

As a result, reformers and conservatives alike can seek their political goals through legal changes without disturbing the notions that the law is a group of abstract principles and that the law, the legal process, and the judges are shielded from partisan politics. Indeed, when the courts fail to rule appropriately, those seeking change (or seeking to prevent change) accuse the judges of failing to apply the law correctly or of making rather than applying it for "political" rather than legal reasons. Each side in such disputes appeals to precedents and the intent of the legislation or to constitutional principles to support its position. Neither has to admit that law is more than a careful deduction from a set of principles, and, therefore, neither must admit that good legal arguments might support very different conclusions for different political rather than purely legal reasons.[4]

4. My point was clearly revealed in the recent debate over Judge Robert Bork's nomination to the U.S. Supreme Court. His opponents charged that Bork's legal writings while an academic and his decisions while on the federal bench revealed that his political views on affirmative action, abortion, and other matters led him to misread and twist the law, making him an inappropriate candidate for a position on the nation's highest court. His supporters insisted that Bork's reading of the law was correct and that his elevation to the Supreme Court would help to reverse a dangerous tendency in the existing court to make rather than apply the law. Each side in the debate accused the other of playing politics, while each vehemently denied the charge. As a result, each could preserve the fiction that law was (or should be) above politics, but of course the debate revealed that it was not. The debate

Although the language and ideology of the law and legal education and practice emphasize fundamental ideas and largely ignore—indeed, deny—the relationship between law and political economy, most legal historians know better, and they seek to trace the connections between social and economic change and the development of the law. Recognizing the existence of connections between law and society is one thing; providing an adequate analysis of that connection is quite another and has produced a lively debate among legal historians. The dominant view among historians is what Robert W. Gordon has called "evolutionary functionalism,"[5] which in its various guises—and this variation is the source of most of the debate—holds that the law is intimately connected to the society of which it is a part in a cause-and-effect relationship: society, broadly speaking, has certain needs

---

centered on political issues and took place in a political arena, the Senate; it seldom included carefully crafted legal arguments but instead centered on the political import of the conclusions Bork had reached in his writings and decisions and how such decisions would affect the Supreme Court if he were a member. Even if each side had presented carefully crafted legal arguments, they would not have resolved the debate. Good legal arguments could be made by either side without being convincing to the other side because the debate was political and not legal.

5. Robert W. Gordon, "Critical Legal Histories," *Stanford Law Review,* 36 (January, 1984), 57–125. Gordon's long essay is a superb analysis of the debate in its various forms and varieties and includes a discussion of "critical legal theory," a view that its adherents claim departs from evolutionary functionalism. A shorter but equally valuable analysis from a very different perspective is James Willard Hurst, "The State of Legal History," *Reviews in American History,* X (December, 1982), 292–305. On critical legal history and theory, see David Kairys, (ed.), *The Politics of Law: A Progressive Critique* (Rev. ed; New York, 1990) and Mark Kelman, *A Guide to Critical Legal Studies* (Cambridge, 1987). Both books show, among other things, that the variation among critical legal theorists is so great that it is easier to see what they oppose than what they favor. A perceptive critique of the Kelman volume is Eugene D. Genovese, "Critical Legal Studies as Radical Politics and World View," *Yale Journal of Law and the Humanities,* III (Winter, 1991), 131–56. I have also found the following to be especially useful: Lawrence M. Friedman, *A History of American Law* (New York, 1973); Lawrence M. Friedman, *Contract Law in America: A Social and Economic Case Study* (Madison, 1965); James Willard Hurst, *Law and Social Order in the United States* (Ithaca, N.Y., 1977); Mark Tushnet, "A Marxist Analysis of American Law," *Marxist Perspectives,* I (Spring, 1978), 96–116; *Law in American History,* Vol. 5 of *Perspectives in American History,* ed. Donald Fleming and Bernard Bailyn (Cambridge, Mass., 1971), a volume of original essays; Morton J. Horwitz, *The Transformation of American Law, 1780–1860* (Cambridge, 1977); Elizabeth Fox-Genovese and Eugene D. Genovese, "Jurisprudence and Property Relations in Bourgeois and Slave Society," *Fruits of Merchant Capital: Slavery and Bourgeois Property in the Rise and Expansion of Capitalism* (New York, 1983), 337–87.

as it evolves and changes, and the law responds to these needs; of course, the law has its own set of rules and processes that profoundly influence its development, and therefore the cause-and-effect relationship is always inexact.

Debate arises among legal historians because this dominant view can and does encompass a great variety of historical interpretations ranging from the notion that the law responds to the needs of an evolving, modernizing society, facilitating and supporting necessary changes and solving problems that arise in the modernization process, to a more purely class-based interpretation that sees the law as a key means whereby a dominant group or class achieves its goals and legitimates its dominant position at the expense of other groups or classes.

In its most formalist form, the notion of law as a response to the needs of a modernizing society meshes easily with the traditional view that law is autonomous and apolitical. If one assumes that society evolves in a certain way—in the Whiggish view, toward modern liberal capitalism, or for our purposes here, toward a free labor society—then the law merely responds to such changes by clearing away inappropriate hindrances to this evolution and by providing statutes and opinions that facilitate it. The relationship between society and the law remains, but the cause-and-effect relationship is blurred, and politics is largely irrelevant, affecting timing and details but not ultimate results. The law and other institutions merely evolve toward a particular goal, propelled by the inner dynamics of the social system. Because this view fits easily with traditional legal thought, it is often an underlying assumption in many judicial opinions.

Ordinarily, judges do not make their assumptions concerning social change explicit and do not include social, political, or economic justifications in their opinions. In keeping with the notion that the task of the court is to discover and apply the law and not make it, judges justify their rulings by considering the intent of relevant legislation and any established legal precedents. In a decision rendered in its April term, 1883, the South Carolina Supreme Court departed from this general practice. After carefully describing the rights of landowners, tenants, and croppers under the lien laws based upon its reading of the intent of laws it analyzed, the court then added its views of the social and economic goals that the laws were designed to achieve, thereby providing both an additional justification for its opinion and an explanation for the evolution of postbellum southern law.[6]

6. Carpenter v. Strickland, 20 South Carolina 1 (1883).

The case, an appeal brought by a landowner against his tenant, really concerned croppers and the lien laws. In January, 1882, B. F. Strickland rented about fifty acres of land from A. A. Carpenter. Strickland then entered into a written agreement with G. W. Wilson to grow cotton and corn on twenty acres of this land, the work to be done "under the direction, supervision and control" of Strickland, who would furnish equipment and half the fertilizer needed and pay Wilson half of the crops produced. Although Strickland had hired him, Wilson received supplies from the landowner, Carpenter, to whom he provided a lien on his share of the crop to be grown. In April, Wilson left the farm and the crops he had planted after having run up a bill for supplies amounting to $82.28. Strickland finished the work on the farm and paid his rent to Carpenter, but he refused to pay the $82.28 Wilson owed Carpenter. Carpenter, claiming that Strickland had verbally agreed to assume Wilson's debt, received a warrant from the clerk of a lower court to seize some of the cotton in Strickland's hands to pay Wilson's debt. Strickland then filed suit to get the cotton returned, arguing that he did not agree to assume Wilson's debt, but in any event he could not be liable for the debt because Wilson was merely a hired laborer and therefore could not give a lien on a crop. The lower court agreed, and Carpenter appealed.

In its decision, the supreme court declared that the clerk of the lower court who had ordered the cotton seized had "exceeded his authority, under the statute." Even if Strickland had verbally agreed to pay Wilson's debt —which Strickland denied—the agreement had no legal validity because under South Carolina law it had to be in writing. This narrow ruling would have settled the matter, and ordinarily appellate courts seek the narrowest grounds necessary to resolve the controversies before them. But in this case, the court decided to go further. Its opinion clarified the lien law and the law concerning croppers and also provided an explicit ideological and economic justification for the laws.

The evidence, the court declared, showed that Wilson was a cropper; although he was to be paid from the proceeds of the crop he grew, "Wilson, under his contract with Strickland, was nothing more than a laborer employed for wages." This simply reiterated established law in South Carolina and elsewhere differentiating a cropper from a tenant. Because Wilson was merely a cropper, the court continued, "we think it follows that he had no right to give a lien upon the crop to be made." This conclusion, it will be recalled, was the subject of some legal controversy. The revised lien laws in every southern state subordinated the cropper's right to his share (that is, to his wages) to the landlord's lien for rent and advances, and the courts had ruled everywhere that the cropper had neither ownership nor control of the crop he produced, including that portion that would eventually be his in payment for his work, until the employer divided the crop. Furthermore, a cropper who voluntarily abandoned his crop, as Wilson apparently did, forfeited his wages. These limitations made lending to the cropper uncertain and risky unless the landlord waived his lien rights or guaranteed payment of the cropper's loans. Nevertheless, the statutes did not explicitly deny the cropper's right to give a lien on that portion that would be his once the division had been made. The South Carolina court apparently decided to settle this matter.

After quoting the law that entitled anyone providing advances "to any person or persons who are employed or about to engage in the cultivation of the soil" a lien on the crop produced for such advances, the court gave its interpretation of the meaning of the law and the intent of the lawmakers who wrote it:

> As we understand it, this means a cultivator of the soil upon his own account; that is to say, a proprietor, either as land owner or tenant, and as such owner of the crop to be made. It could not have been the intention of the law to include a mere laborer for wages, although he might be engaged as a farm hand in the cultivation of the soil.

In short, the court declared, the intent of the legislature was to give farmers the security they needed to get credit; the lawmakers did not expect the law to allow workers to get that credit.

Again, this would have settled matters. Because Wilson was merely a cropper—that is, a hired worker and not "a cultivator of the soil upon his own account"—he could not give a lien. Therefore, Carpenter's claim was lost.[7] But the court then went on to justify its reading of the law by describ-

---

7. In later decisions the court repeated its insistence that a cropper could not give a lien; it made no difference whether his wages were in money or in a share of the crop. See Richey & Miller v. DuPre, 20 South Carolina 6 (1883); McCutchen v. Cranshaw *et al.*, 40 South Carolina 511, 19 S.E. 140 (1894).

ing the intent of the legislature in much broader terms: "the laborer has no interest in the crop as such, and to authorize him to encumber the crop of his employer would be to give him rights in the property of another, to introduce great confusion, and, indeed, to destroy the important business of farming with hired labor."

The court couched both its legal and its social justifications in what appear to be strictly legal terms. Its analysis of the language in the statute and the intent of the legislature provided legal justification for concluding that a cropper, because he was simply a wage laborer, could not give a lien on the crop he worked to produce. When the court then added that to decide otherwise would undermine property rights, introduce "confusion," and interfere with using hired labor in agriculture, it implied that the language of the law and the intent of the legislature that passed it specifically sought to avoid such problems.

The underlying, if unstated, assumption was that the laws enacted by the legislature and interpreted by the courts defined the rights of workers, tenants, and employers and resolved unforeseen problems that arose in an effort to build a free labor society to replace the slave society. Thus the court could claim that it was not making the law but simply discovering it and applying it to the case at hand when it found that the intent and the language of the lien law and the law concerning the status of croppers was to end "confusion" and to promote the "important business of farming with hired labor."

The South Carolina court's views offer a plausible interpretation of the evolution of postbellum southern law that I have described in previous chapters. Emancipation required new laws to govern production with hired labor, and the South Carolina legislature, the court insisted, enacted the necessary laws intending to avoid any confusion and to facilitate the development of a free labor system, a system, the court implied, that would be similar to that in the North. Indeed, this is what seems to have happened. In its essentials, postbellum southern law differed little from that in the North, and it supported a free labor system in the South that in important respects was similar to that in the North. The law that stipulated that the cropper was a wage laborer paid in kind meant that employers of croppers could exercise complete managerial control, determining what would be grown, the seed, fertilizer, tools, and work animals to be used, the hours and pace of work, and even the time and price of the sale of the croppers' shares. In short, the law made it possible to make the croppers part of a rural proletariat on the pattern of the industrial proletariat in the North. Croppers, like northern workers, had a legal right to their wages but no legal right to the goods they produced and from which their wages would come; in both sections, employers owned the means of production, and they, not the employees, made all management decisions.

Tenancy law in the South also followed the northern pattern. Southern tenants, like those in the North, were legally obligated to pay their rents and the debts they contracted. Lenders in both sections could get mortgages and liens on the property of borrowers to secure their loans; crop liens were far more common in the South, where the only security most borrowers could offer was property still to be produced, a special case arising from wartime losses and emancipation.

The southern landlords' control over the private, nonworking lives of their workers seems much greater than that exercised by northern employers, but this difference must be evaluated with caution. Northern employers did not lack that control because they failed to try to achieve it. Paying workers in scrip redeemable only at a company store was not unique to southern plantation owners; and Andrew Carnegie, John D. Rockefeller, and George Pullman, to give but three well-known examples, built company towns in which they owned the land, the houses, the recreational facilities, and even the churches, and they used this ownership as a weapon to control their employees' working and private lives.

Although southern law concerning tenancy was similar to that in the North, it included enough limitations on tenants to enable landowners who so desired to treat them much as they did the croppers and thereby transform both croppers and tenants into a rural proletariat. In places, this is exactly what happened, a development the Census Bureau recognized in 1910 in a special study of what it called "tenant plantations." These were large-scale, centrally organized business operations that were not simply groups of small independent tenant farmers renting from a single landlord. Indeed, the term *tenant plantations* was itself a misnomer, for the workers on such plantations were usually croppers, not tenants, but even when they were legally tenants, the bureau study showed that they were not treated as such.[8]

8. "Plantations in the South," U.S. Bureau of Census, *Thirteenth Census,* 1910: *Agriculture,* Chapter XII. The bureau published an expanded version of this chapter separately

Managers on these plantations supervised all the work and made all management decisions concerning the production and sale of the crops. Such was the plantation Trail Lake, owned and operated by William Alexander Percy. Percy employed both tenants and croppers. Although he called both his "partners" in a "profit-sharing" enterprise, these so-called partners worked under the close supervision of resident managers, and they received not a share of the profits but payment for work done. Even those who might be legally classified as tenants rather than croppers received the same treatment, the only difference being that their pay was higher. The "partnership-contract," Percy wrote, recognized two types of workers, the majority (124 of the 149 families) who were propertyless and the rest who owned their "stock and equipment." In language that clearly indicated that he treated both as nothing more than wage workers, Percy explained that the contract with those with their own stock and equipment "differs from the other only in giving three-fourths instead of one-half of the yield to the tenant." On "settlement day" at the end of the season, both received a cash payment based upon the value of the cotton they had grown less the value of goods taken from the plantation store during the year.[9]

The significance of Percy's Trail Lake plantation was that it was typical of those described in the 1910 Census Bureau study, typical of what may be called modern business plantations similarly organized in many areas of the South. On such plantations, a tenant was simply a cropper with a mule, and both tenants and croppers were part of a new agricultural proletariat. And almost without exception, this agricultural proletariat of tenants, croppers, and wage workers on the business plantations were African-Americans.[10]

The development of Trail Lake and similar business plantations would seem to support the South Carolina court's view that the intent of the lien laws and the laws concerning croppers—and by extension the laws so lim-

---

in 1916: U.S. Bureau of Census, *Plantation Farming in the United States* (Washington, D.C., 1916). The census, seemingly oblivious to the laws, made no distinction between tenants and croppers until 1920, and even then merely listed croppers as a special, southern form of tenancy.

    9. William Alexander Percy, *Lanterns on the Levee: Recollections of a Planter's Son* (1941; rpr. Baton Rouge, 1973), 275–76, 278, 290–91.

    10. Harold D. Woodman, "The Reconstruction of the Cotton Plantation in the New South," in *Essays on the Postbellum Southern Economy,* eds. Thavolia Glymph and John J. Kushma (College Station, Tex., 1985), 95–119.

iting the rights of tenants as to allow them to be treated as little more than croppers—was to promote the "important business of farming with hired labor." It would follow, therefore, that changes in the law, either through statute or court interpretation, were simply aimed, as the court put it, to avoid "confusion" as the economy and the law evolved towards bourgeois labor relations on the plantations.

But the business plantations did not develop everywhere in the postbellum agricultural South. A very different kind of agricultural South arose in those areas where the business plantations did not exist. In the same year that Percy published his *Lanterns on the Levee*, another observer, James Agee, described that other South. *Let Us Now Praise Famous Men* is Agee's report on the visit he and Walker Evans had made to Alabama in 1936. In it, he appended "A Definition" in which he described the difference between a tenant and a sharecropper. Both, he reported, were landless tenants, but southerners reserved the term *tenant* to refer to a man who "owns a mule and some farm implements and who, not needing to be furnished these, can arrange to yield less of his two major crops in payment of rent to the landowner." The tenant who "owning neither mule nor implements, must be furnished these as well as land and shelter, must pay the landowner half his cotton and a third to half his corn, is a sharecropper."[11]

The difference in the language used by Percy and Agee to describe the distinction between a tenant and a cropper obscures the legal distinction but clearly reveals the difference in practice. Workers on Percy's Trail Lake plantation *received* more if they used their own mules and equipment; those in the areas Agee visited *paid* less for the use of the land if they owned mules and equipment. In areas such as Agee visited, primarily in the hill country where the majority of the population was white and where the land was less fertile and productive, the business plantations did not exist. In these areas, traditional tenant-landlord relations persisted, and, as Agee correctly noted, the cropper was simply a tenant without a mule and therefore had to pay a higher rent because his landlord provided the mule and equipment. Most of the landowners in the hill country operated small farms and sought

11. James Agee and Walker Evans, *Let Us Now Praise Famous Men* (Boston, 1941), 454–55. Alabama, it will be recalled, abolished the distinction between a cropper and a tenant after 1923, making both tenants. See pp. 74–75, above. Elsewhere, while the distinction remained, in practice in the nonplantation areas, croppers and tenants were often treated as tenants.

to increase their incomes by renting any lands they could not work themselves to others—some black, but most white—and the landowners, like their tenants, looked to local merchants to get the supplies they needed to plant and gather a crop. Absentee landlords and local merchants often owned large parcels of land that they subdivided and rented in small units to tenants. Lien laws protected the landowner's rent, but in practice they often offered greater protection to the merchant lender who, as the years went by, through foreclosures and purchases gradually became the largest landowner in the area and enjoyed all the protection that the laws afforded landlords.

Thus the evidence would seem to support the view that the law was simply a response to the needs of the postemancipation society evolving into a free labor system, and that the particular economic and social relations that finally emerged were therefore somehow the inevitable results of creating that free labor system. This explanation is inadequate, however, because it minimizes the role of the actors in the story by simply assuming that the laws and, more important, the particular results they produced were the inevitable responses to social forces generated by building a free labor society. In a word, the explanation is inadequate because it leaves out politics, the politics of electioneering and of engineering laws through the legislature but also, more generally, the politics of power and the changing configuration of power distribution over time.

We may begin to add politics to the story by returning to the South Carolina court's 1883 opinion. The court's description of the intent of the lien laws was correct, but only in a limited sense. The aim of the statutes in South Carolina and elsewhere in the South was to enable farmers in a war-devastated economy to get the credit they needed. The credit needs of the former slaveowners were particularly pressing because emancipation at once destroyed the planters' most valuable form of security for loans (which made a new form of security a necessity) and left them no choice but to employ workers (which increased their operating costs and their need for credit).

It is doubtful, however, that the planters and their representatives in the state legislatures intended the creation of a free labor market that would facilitate "the important business of farming with hired labor" because it is doubtful that they fully understood what the creation of such a market entailed. The passage of the black codes and anti-enticement legislation and the use of violence and intimidation as a means to control a labor force that they were convinced would never work except under compulsion suggest that the planters had in mind a very restricted and coerced labor system closely resembling slavery rather than the free labor system that existed elsewhere in the country.

As we have seen and as the South Carolina court noted, the conservative, planter-dominated legislatures that passed the first lien laws certainly did not expect them to enable the freedmen to secure credit and escape control by their former owners. On the contrary, they expected that the laws that provided planters with the means to get the credit would enable them to hold on to their land and to reestablish the control over their work force that emancipation had ended. The only credit the workers might receive would be an advance on their wages, the extent and the amount to be determined by the employers, an arrangement that would strengthen, not weaken, employer control. The planters anticipated that delayed wage payments would force workers to remain on the job until the end of the year, and because workers would need advances on their withheld wages throughout the year, employers could keep them dependent and therefore docile throughout the year.

Besides providing a means to control the work force, this arrangement also decreased the amount of cash needed if workers were paid at regular intervals. It could also become an additional source of income for the planters. As Barbara J. Fields has perceptively noted, delayed wage payments really amounted to the workers granting year-long credit to their employers. In return for advances on wages already earned but not yet paid, the workers not only received no interest, but instead had to pay interest on purchases they had no choice but to make on credit.[12]

Understandably enough, the former slaves resisted this arrangement, but their resistance did not mean that they had a better understanding of "the important business of farming with hired labor." If they clearly recognized that the planters sought a system that differed little from slavery, the free labor system envisioned by the northern victors did not seem much better. The freedom to enter into contracts to work in a manner that did not differ materially from work regimes under slavery seemed to mock the meaning of the word. Their hopes to get land of their own, their refusal to

12. Barbara J. Fields, "The Advent of Capitalist Agriculture: The New South in a Bourgeois World," in *Essays on the Postbellum Southern Economy,* eds. Glymph and Kushma, 86–87.

work in gangs under overseers, their demands for prompt regular payment of wages, and their efforts to find sources of credit other than their employers, to become tenants or to become partners rather than employees—all were attempts to escape dependence on their former owners and to give what they considered to be real meaning to their freedom.

Although the South Carolina court suggested that the legal change was a response to the creation of a new system to replace the old, in practice legal changes came piecemeal in response to particular, usually unanticipated problems as they arose. If emancipation made significant legal change inevitable, the precise nature of that change and therefore the results were far from inevitable. At every stage in the development of the law, the path chosen was not the only one available to solve a newly recognized problem. Indeed, the very recognition that a problem existed and, more important, what that problem was, helped to determine if and how the problem would be solved. Freedmen who found themselves deprived of their wages because their employers refused to pay them or because their employers could not pay them after paying other debts recognized a problem that was of little moment to their employers. But when the freedmen received help from the Freedmen's Bureau at the expense of employers and merchants or used existing law to carve out a measure of independence by creating competition between employers and merchants or succeeded in getting laborers' lien laws that had priority over all other debts of their employers, planters and merchants considered the results to be new problems to be solved, while the freedmen considered them to be solutions to problems they faced.

In the course of recognizing certain conditions as problems and then seeking to solve them, the postbellum southern legislatures and courts built the legal support for a system that defined the rights of workers, tenants, and employers, helping to create in the process a new dominant agricultural class of landowning planters and merchants ruling over a subordinate group of small farmers and tenants and a largely black rural proletariat. These results were not foreordained. No abstract economic necessity demanded that the southern rural proletariat be forced into the helpless, low-paid, dependent position it came to occupy or that increasing numbers of small farmers in the nonplantation areas gradually lose their land and become dependent, poverty-stricken tenants. Adding the political dimension provides the missing explanatory insights. But adding politics to the story of the evolution of the law is no easy matter.

Some legal theorists and historians have added politics to legal history by arguing that in a society characterized by class and racial divisions as well as by many other interest-group differences, "interest bargaining through law" becomes an accepted means to resolve the conflicts and legitimize the legal process. But because some groups lack sufficient political power, adequate organization, or a clear recognition of their interests, they do not have equal access to the "bargaining arena," and as a result those groups that *do* have access to the bargaining arena can bend the law to serve their particular interests at the expense of others. From this, some conclude that the law is a means whereby a ruling elite establishes, maintains, and legitimates its control.

Despite its sometimes crude and deterministic application,[13] this view of the law provides powerful interpretive insights into the evolution of postbellum law in the South. It directs attention to the people involved, their varying perceptions of goals to be achieved, and their varying attempts to achieve such goals. Instead of being the inevitable result of forces or needs inherent in an evolving free labor system, the new law was the result of efforts to impose rules of the game based upon competing and often contradictory visions of what those rules should be—in short, as a result of class conflict involving landowners, freedmen, merchants, and tenants.

When viewed from this perspective and from the end of the story, the evolution of the legal changes in the South after the Civil War seems clearly to be the result of a resurgent landowning class being able to impose its will on helpless freedmen and a new merchant class able to impose its will on small landowners and tenants. But to argue that the law was simply the means used by the ruling class of landowners and merchants to achieve such ends simultaneously says both too much and too little—too much, because it assumes that the landowners who survived the war were united and had

13. In its crudest form, this view has a nice inner logic that defies its being questioned. When legislation or a court decision clearly favors the ruling class, it becomes proof of the interpretation, but when the law protects the ruled or limits the power of the rulers, then it becomes a clever means used by the ruling class to fool the ruled by making them believe that the law is fair and objective. Among other problems with this very narrow view of the law, as James Willard Hurst has perceptively noted, is that it cannot adequately account for change, it must dismiss as unimportant those aspects of the law that protect and promote the goals and values of interests other than those of the ruling elite, and it must assume a monolithic ruling class with identical interests that it fully recognizes and has the ability to impose upon legislatures, courts, and administrative agencies. Hurst, "The State of Legal History."

a clear vision of the kind of system they ultimately developed; and too little, because it begs the question of how and why they were so successful.

In the immediate aftermath of the Civil War, former planters, former slaves, merchants, and small farmers had different visions of the future which, in the course of attempting to turn visions into reality, often produced sharp conflicts. But it would be a mistake to conclude that the redeemers, when they finally gained control of the political and legal arena, were able to impose the planters' vision on the rest of southern society. In the first place, conditions that finally emerged did not fully conform to what planters had in mind at the start, but included concessions to merchants and to the workers. But even more important is that the planters' vision of a free labor system, like that of their former slaves, was based on their experience with a slave labor system, the only experience most of them ever had. The conflicts surfacing in 1865 continued but changed amidst the varying attempts to recognize and resolve problems, gradually producing in the process a free labor system in the agricultural South and a new ruling class of landowners and merchants. The law provided the new rules of the game, but equally important, the law provided the ideological justification for those new rules, and did so in language that hid the class basis for the new rules and made them appear universal. Thus the South Carolina court in 1882 could declare that the laws concerning cropper and tenant labor were necessary for the "important business of farming with hired labor" and, ignoring the political struggle and ensuing compromises, rule that it was the intent of the legislature when they wrote the original laws to create the system as it had developed by 1882.

In fact, at each step in the development, there were possible alternative steps that were not taken.[14] The confiscation of planters' land and its distribution to the former slaves has been the usual alternative path that historians have raised and debated. But short of such a massive change in property relations in the South—which, in any event, would have required changes in federal rather than state laws—many other alternatives were possible, some of which might have led to property redistribution without the radical implications of confiscation. If, for example, the law required that work-

14. Obviously, to suggest possible alternatives puts the historian in the dangerous realm of counterfactual conjecture. What-if history, if combined with enough assumptions, makes any conceivable alternative possible. Nevertheless, if we pose our assumptions with care, we can gain some insight into how the law evolved in the way it did.

ers be paid in cash at regular intervals (rather than at the end of the season) and if payment of workers' wages took precedence over all other debts including rents, landowners might have been forced to sell portions of their lands to pay debts and wage obligations; falling land values would then make purchase easier for those receiving cash wages.[15]

When the freedmen forced planters to divide their property into smaller tracts worked by squads or families, the results may have been quite different from the way in which they actually evolved. Those who became tenants might have retained far more of the traditional tenant's rights. In areas where sharecropping evolved, the courts might have ruled that the relationship created was not one of employer-employee but rather, as some freedmen insisted, a partnership that gave both partners a share in management decisions and in the profits earned. If the courts failed to rule in this way, new statutes could have accomplished the same end.

A comparison between conditions in the North and the South offers additional insights into alternative paths not taken in the evolution of southern law. Land and other property were not distributed to immigrants and other landless agricultural workers in the North, but the results in the North were quite different from those in the South. Presumably northern employers would have preferred a docile, low-paid, dependent labor force, and indeed they did their best to get such a labor force by building company towns, by firing and blacklisting those who complained and agitated about low wages, sought to organize unions, or in any way caused trouble, and by using legal means such as the labor injunction or extralegal force to break strikes and intimidate workers. Nevertheless, northern employers made significantly greater concessions to their employees than did southern employers in the form of higher pay, shorter hours, and better working conditions without giving up their dominant economic position. Of course, North-South comparisons must avoid romanticizing conditions in the North. Low wages, long hours, unhealthful and dangerous working conditions, recurrent unemployment, slum housing—the conditions that led workers to call their condition "wage slavery" and that stimulated the rise of trade unions and the zealous efforts of reformers—should provide ample warning that comparisons be made with care. Nevertheless, the differences between conditions in the two sections are significant.

15. This is how Edward Atkinson envisioned the future of the free labor South. See Atkinson, "The Future Supply of Cotton," *North American Review,* XCVIII (April, 1864), 477–97.

Finally, a revealing picture of alternative paths not taken may be seen in changes in southern agriculture during the past half century. Sharecropping has disappeared, as has most small-scale tenancy, and race relations have radically altered. New statutes and different rulings on existing statutes have created a very different agricultural South from that which grew up in the eight decades following the Civil War.

In short, if capitalist social relations have similar laws concerning property and labor relations, similar laws do not produce identical results. Indeed, identical laws may produce very different results, or, to be more precise, what appear to be identical laws are not really the same. Politics, the ability to exercise control, explains why the planters were able to achieve as much as they did and why the southern system became so much more repressive than that in the North or that in the South since the Civil Rights movement.

On the most obvious level, changes in the law that added or decreased the rights and obligations of workers and tenants directly paralleled changes in politics. Thus, it will be recalled, new statutes that provided additional protection to landlords for rent and advances and that subordinated the rights of workers to their wages to the rights of landlords invariably followed immediately after the victory of the redeemers. Similarly, workers received the greatest protection from the Freedmen's Bureau and from the legislatures and courts during the radical period in each state. In the South, unlike the North, violence and intimidation followed by formal laws disfranchising blacks (and many poor whites as well) deprived them of a key means to encourage change and reform.

In the end, the postemancipation laws supported the creation of two quite different new agricultural Souths. In both, some laborers, croppers, and tenants dreamed of climbing the agricultural ladder. But for most members of the agricultural proletariat, there was no ladder to climb. Their meager incomes made buying a mule and equipment difficult and buying land next to impossible. The best most could hope for was a more decent employer—or work in the city. Some managed to buy some equipment and rise into the ranks of tenants, and some even managed to buy land, but they, like those in the nonplantation areas, found their new position on the agricultural ladder precarious. Its rickety structure made climbing difficult, and its broken rungs more often than not caused those attempting to climb instead to fall.

A planter such as William Alexander Percy could call the tenants and croppers who worked on his plantation his profit-sharing partners, but he and those who worked for him knew full well that they were neither. Percy owned the land and most of the equipment and made all the managerial decisions—hardly a sign of a partnership—and he paid his workers according to what they produced—a piece-work arrangement, not profit sharing. That in 1941 he felt it necessary to defend his arrangement with his workers in the ways he did reflected the growing challenge to the system that his grandfather, his father, and he had built. Ironically, the challenge that would soon destroy the legal and ideological basis for his economic and political power would be in part a legal challenge which, although it would include new statutes, would come from a new interpretation of existing statutes and constitutional provisions. The movement from Plessy to Brown illustrates how the law can bring significant change and reform, even as it maintains its conservatism with each side finding ample precedents to support its position.

Cases Cited

Alabama

Bailey v. State, 158 Alabama 18, 48 So. 498 (1908), 92
Beard v. Woodward, 78 Alabama 317 (1884), 57
Bell v. Hurst, 75 Alabama 44 (1883), 57, 58
Boyett v. Potter, 80 Alabama 476, 2 South 534 (1887), 57
Coleman v. Siler, 74 Alabama 435 (1883), 58
Comer v. Daniel, 69 Alabama 434 (1881), 57
Connor v. Jackson, 74 Alabama 464 (1883), 57
Dulany v. Dickerson, 12 Alabama 601 (1847), 11
Foster v. Napier, 74 Alabama 393 (1883), 58
Foxworth v. Brown *et al.,* 120 Alabama 59, 24 So. 1 (1898), 65
Gardner v. Head, 108 Alabama 619, 18 So. 551 (1895), 79
Heaton v. Slaton *et al.,* 141 So. 267 (Alabama, 1932), 75
Marcus v. Robinson, 76 Alabama 550 (1884), 57
Schuessler v. Gains, 68 Alabama 556 (1881), 57
Smith v. Tankersley, 20 Alabama 213 (1852), 74
Stewart v. Young, 212 Alabama 426, 103 So. 44 (1925), 75
Toney v. State, 141 Alabama 120 (1904), 91
Watson v. Auerbach, 57 Alabama 353 (1876), 57

Arkansas

Adams v. Hobbs, 27 Arkansas 1 (1871), 60
Airey v. Weinstein, 54 Arkansas 443, 16 S.W. 123 (1891), 61
Barnhardt v. State, 169 Arkansas 567, 275 S.W. 909 (1925), 69
Bigham v. Cropss, 69 Arkansas 581, 65 S.W. 101 (1901), 61
Bourland *et al.* v. McKnight & Bros., 79 Arkansas 427, 96 S.W. 179 (1906), 61, 69

Buck v. Lee, 36 Arkansas 525 (1880), 60
Burgie v. Davis, 34 Arkansas 179 (1879), 79
Christian v. Crocker *et al.*, 25 Arkansas 327 (1869), 68, 77
Crawford v. Slaten, 155 Arkansas 283, 244 S.W. 32 (1922), 80
Earl Bros. & Co. v. Malone, 80 Arkansas 218, 96 S.W. 1062 (1906), 61
Ferniman v. Nowlin, 91 Arkansas 20, 120 S.W. 378 (1909), 61
Franklin v. Meyer, 36 Arkansas 96 (1880), 60
Hammock v. Creekmore, 48 Arkansas 264, 3 S.W. 180 (1887), 69
Hibbard v. Kirby, 38 Arkansas 102 (1881), 80
Johnson v. Mantooth, 108 Arkansas 36, 156 S.W. 448 (1913), 69
Lambeth v. Ponder, 33 Arkansas 707 (1878), 60
Latham v. Barwick, 87 Arkansas 328, 113 S.W. 646 (1908), 80
Meyer v. Bloom, 37 Arkansas 43 (1881), 60
Ponder v. Rhea, 32 Arkansas 435 (1877), 69, 72, 90
Rand v. Walton, 130 Arkansas 431, 197 S.W. 852 (1917), 80
Roth v. Williams, 45 Arkansas 447 (1885), 61
Sentell v. Moore, 34 Arkansas 687 (1879), 69
Sheeks-Stephen Store Co. v. Richardson, 76 Arkansas 282, 88 S.W. 983 (1905), 79
Smith v. Myer and Bro., 25 Arkansas 609 (1869), 60
Somers v. Musolf, 86 Arkansas 97, 109 S.W. 1173 (1908), 84
Tinsley v. Craige, 54 Arkansas 346, 16 S.W. 570 (1891), 61
Tomlinson v. Greenfield, 31 Arkansas 557 (1876), 60
Varner v. Rice, 39 Arkansas 344 (1882), 61
Watson v. Johnson, 33 Arkansas 737 (1878), 60
Watson v. May, 62 Arkansas 435, 35 S.W. 1108 (1896), 79
Woodson *et ux.* v. McLaughlin *et al.*, 150 Arkansas 340, 234 S.W. 185 (1921), 84

FLORIDA

Patterson v. Taylor, 15 Florida 336 (1875), 58
Weed v. Standley, 12 Florida 166 (1868), 58

GEORGIA

Alexander & Howell v. Edmund Glenn *et al.*, 39 Georgia 1 (1869), 33
Almond v. Scott, 80 Georgia 95, 4 S.E. 892 (1888), 69
Alston v. Wilson, 64 Georgia 482 (1880), 79
Appling v. Odom and Mercier, 46 Georgia 583 (1872), 68, 70, 90
Boyce v. Day, 3 Georgia App. 275, 95 S.E. 930 (1907), 44
Brimberry v. Mansfield, 86 Georgia 792, 13 S.E. 132 (1891), 43
Bussell v. Bishop, 152 Georgia 428, 110 S.E. 174 (1921), 83
Byrd & Crocker v. H. R. Johnson & Co., 38 Georgia 113 (1868), 29, 30
Clark & Cole v. Miles G. Dobbins *et al.*, 52 Georgia 656 (1874), 36
DeLoach *et al.* v. Delk, 119 Georgia 884, 47 S.E. 204 (1904), 69
Elliott v. Parker, 94 Georgia 620, 20 S.E. 106 (1894), 43

Fargason v. Ford, 119 Georgia 343, 46 S.E. 431 (1904), 44

Fields v. Harris, 34 Georgia App. 445, 129 S.E. 664 (1925), 69

Fortune v. Braswell, 139 Georgia 609, 77 S.E. 818 (1913), 91

Fountain v. Fountain, 10 Georgia App. 758, 73 S.E. 1096 (1912), 88

Gardner v. Smith, 39 Georgia App. 224 (1929), 81

Gurr v. Martin, 73 Georgia 528 (1884), 77

Harvey v. Lewis, 19 Georgia App. 655, 91 S.E. 1052 (1917), 80, 84

Henderson v. Hughes, 4 Georgia App. 52, 60 S.E. 813 (1908), 45

Holfield & Company v. White, 52 Georgia 567 (1874), 77

Holloway v. Brinkley, 42 Georgia 226 (1871), 77

Johnson v. Emanuel, 50 Georgia 590 (1874), 32, 35

Kellam v. State, 2 Georgia App. 479, 58 S.E. 695 (1907), 42

Lamar v. State, 120 Georgia 312, 47 S.E. 958 (1904), 92

Lewis v. Owens, 124 Georgia 228, 52 S.E. 333 (1905), 82

McCook v. Cousins, 39 Georgia 125 (1869), 34

McElmurray v. Turner, 86 Georgia 212, 12 S.E. 358 (1890), 69

McGarr v. State, 13 Georgia App. 80, 78 S.E. 776 (1913), 42

Morrison v. State, 111 Georgia 642, 36 S.E. 902 (1900), 42

Payne v. Trammell, 29 Georgia App. 475, 115 S.E. 923 (1923), 81

Phillips v. Freeman, 30 Georgia App. 450, 118 S.E. 104 (1923), 44

Polk v. Thomason, 130 Georgia 542, 61 S.E. 123 (1908), 91

Reece v. State, 5 Georgia App. 663, 63 S.E. 690 (1909), 42

Rodgers v. Black, 99 Georgia 139, 25 S.E. 23 (1896), 44

Rousey v. Mattox, 111 Georgia 883, 36 S.E. 925 (1900), 79

Saulsbury, Repess & Company v. S. E. Eason, 47 Georgia 617 (1873), 38

Scott v. Pound, 61 Georgia 579 (1878), 43

Sims v. State, 43 Georgia App. 438, 158 S.E. 913 (1931), 42

Smith v. State, 17 Georgia App. 554, 87 S.E. 829 (1916), 42

Smith v. Summerlin, 48 Georgia 425 (1873), 77

Speer v. Hart, 45 Georgia 113 (1872), 38

Steward v. Hill *et al.,* 134 Georgia 596, 68 S.E. 328 (1910), 91

Swann v. Morris, 83 Georgia 143, 9 S.E. 767 (1889), 43

Thornton v. Carver, 80 Georgia 397, 6 S.E. 915 (1888), 41

Toler *et al.* v. Seabrook, 39 Georgia 14 (1869), 11, 34, 37

Townsend v. State, 124 Georgia 69, 52, S.E. 293 (1905), 92

Ware v. Simmons, 55 Georgia 94 (1875), 36

Wilson v. State, 138 Georgia 489, 75 S.E. 619 (1912), 92

Wyatt v. Turner, 37 Georgia 640 (1868), 29, 30

LOUISIANA

Bres & O'Brien v. S. C. & J. A. Cowan, 22 Louisiana Ann. 438 (1870), 68, 77, 79

Dixon v. Alford, 143 So. 679 (Louisiana App. 1932), 81, 85

Dixon v. Watson, 143, So. 683 (Louisiana App. 1932), 81, 85

Harrison v. Goldberg, 133 Louisiana 389, 63 So. 59 (1913), 81

CASES CITED

Hewitt v. Williams, 47 Louisiana Ann. 742, 17 So. 269 (1895), 56
Holmes v. Payne, 4 Louisiana App. 345 (1926), 69
Jones v. Dowling, 12 Louisiana App. 362, 125 So. 478 (1929), 69
Lalanne Brothers v. McKinney, 28 Louisiana Ann. 642 (1876), 69, 77
Moore v. Gray, 22 Louisiana Ann. 289 (1870), 79
Young v. Gay, 41 Louisiana Ann. 758, 6 So. 608 (1889), 85

MISSISSIPPI

Alexander v. Zeigler, 84 Mississippi 560, 36 So. 536 (1894), 69
Arbuckle v. Nelms, 50 Mississippi 556 (1874), 12, 47
Bain v. Brooks, 46 Mississippi 537 (1872), 46
Betts v. Ratliff, 50 Mississippi 561 (1874), 68
Doctor Doty v. John T. Heth, 52 Mississippi 530 (1876), 46, 47
Deyfus *et al.* v. W. A. Gage & Co., 84 Mississippi 219, 36 So. 248 (1904), 48, 65
Ellis v. Jones, 70 Mississippi 60, 11 So. 566 (1892), 48
French v. Picard, 49 Mississippi 320 (1873), 46
Hollingsworth *et al.* v. Hill *et al.*, 69 Mississippi 73, 10 So. 430 (1891), 79
Howard v. Simmons, 43 Mississippi 75 (1870), 46
Lumbley v. Thomas, 65 Mississippi 97, 5 So. 823 (1887), 69
Millsaps v. Tate, 75 Mississippi 150, 21 So. 663 (1897), 42
Newman *et al.* v. Bank of Greenville *et al.*, 66 Mississippi 323, 5 So. 753 (1889), 48, 65, 79
Paxton v. Meyer, 58 Mississippi 445 (1880), 48
Phillips v. Douglass, 53 Mississippi 175 (1876), 47
Stamps v. Gillman, 43 Mississippi 456 (1870), 46
Stewart v. Hollins *et al.*, 47 Mississippi 708 (1873), 12, 21, 46
Storm v. Green, 51 Mississippi 103 (1875), 47
Taylor v. Nelson, 54 Mississippi 524 (1877), 48
White v. Thomas, 52 Mississippi 49 (1876), 47

NORTH CAROLINA

Brazier v. Ansley, 33 North Carolina 12 (1850), 74
Deaver v. Rice, 20 North Carolina 567 (1839), 14
Denton v. Strickland, 48 North Carolina 61 (1855), 74
Durham v. Speeke, 82 North Carolina 87 (1880), 53
Harrison v. Ricks, 71 North Carolina 7 (1874), 53, 73, 74
Hudgins v. Wood, 72 North Carolina 256 (1875) 89
Parker v. Brown, 136 North Carolina 280, 48 S.E. 657 (1904), 83
Peebles v. Lassiter, 33 North Carolina 73 (1850), 14
Ross v. Swaringer *et al.*, 31 North Carolina 481 (1849), 14
State v. Austin, 123 North Carolina 749, 31 S.E. 731 (1898), 86
State v. Burwell, 63 North Carolina 661 (1869), 69, 74

State v. Jones, 19 North Carolina 544 (1837), 74
State v. Keith, 126 North Carolina 1114, 36 S.E. 169 (1900), 87
Thigpen v. Leigh, 93 North Carolina 47 (1885), 80, 89
Varner v. Spencer *et al.*, 72 North Carolina 381 (1875), 86
Wolston v. Bryan, 64 North Carolina 764 (1870), 74

Oklahoma

Moore *et al.* v. Linn *et al.*, 19 Oklahoma 279, 91 P. 910 (1907), 69
Taylor v. Higgins, 129 Oklahoma 57, 263 P. 146 (1928), 87

South Carolina

Birt v. Greene & Co. *et al.*, 127 South Carolina 70, 120 S.E. 747 (1924), 79
Carpenter v. Strickland, 20 South Carolina 1 (1883), 69, 90, 101
Dunn v. Spears, 5 South Carolina 17 (1873), 49
DuRant v. Home Bank of Barnwell, 129 South Carolina 283, 124 S.E. 12 (1924), 79
Hamilton v. Blanton, 107 South Carolina 142, 92 S.E. 275 (1917), 79
Hardwick v. Page, 124 South Carolina 111, 117 S.E. 204 (1923), 80
Huff v. Watkins, 15 South Carolina 82 (1880), 68–69, 77
Malcolm Mercantile Co. v. Britt, 102 South Carolina 499, 87 S.E. 143 (1915), 69, 87
McCutchen v. Cranshaw *et al.*, 40 South Carolina 511, 19 S.E. 140 (1894), 69, 103
Nexsen v. Ward *et al.*, 96 South Carolina 313, 80 S.E. 599 (1914), 51
People's Bank v. Walker, 132 South Carolina 254, 128 S.E. 715 (1925), 69
Richey & Miller v. DuPre, 20 South Carolina 6 (1883), 77, 90, 103
Salley v. Cox, 94 South Carolina 216, 77 S.E. 933 (1913), 80
State v. Sanders *et al.*, 110 South Carolina 487, 96 S.E. 622 (1918), 86
State v. Saunders, 52 South Carolina 580, 30 S.E. 616 (1898), 85
Sternberger v. McSween, 14 South Carolina 35 (1880), 42
Visanska v. Bradley, 4 South Carolina 288 (1873), 49

Tennessee

Dunlap v. Aycock, 57 Tennessee 561 (1873), 62
Hughes v. Whitaker, 51 Tennessee 399 (1871), 62
Hunt v. Wing *et al.*, 57 Tennessee 139 (1872), 17, 68
Lewis v. Mahon, 68 Tennessee 374 (1878), 62
Mann v. Taylor, 52 Tennessee 267 (1871), 68, 77
Schoenlau-Steiner Trunk Top & Veneer Co. v. Hilderbrand *et al.*, 152 Tennessee 166, 274 S.W. 544 (1925), 61
Thurman v. Jenkins, 61 Tennessee 426 (1873), 62
Whitmore v. Poindexter, 66 Tennessee 248 (1874), 62

Cases Cited

Texas

Barnett v. Govan, 241 S.W. 276 (Texas C.A., 1922), 83
Brown v. Johnson, 118 Texas 143, 12 S.W. (2d.) 543 (1929), 69
Crews v. Cortez, 102 Texas 111, 113 S.W. 523 (1908), 85
Fagan v. Vogt, 35 Texas C.A. 528, 80 S.W. 664 (1904), 85
Horsley v. Moss et al., 5 Texas C.A. 341, 23 S.W. 1115 (1893), 69
Jones v. Avant, 41 Texas 650 (1874), 59
Land et al. v. Roby, 56 Texas C.A. 333, 120 S.W. 1057 (1909), 79
Matthews v. Foster, 238 S.W. 317 (Texas C.A., 1922), 85
McGee v. Fitzer, 37 Texas 27 (1872–73), 59, 69, 90
Rogers v. McGuffey, 96 Texas 565, 74 S.W. 753 (1903), 85
Rupert v. Swindle, 212 S.W. 670 (Texas C.A., 1919), 85
Tignor v. Toney, 13 Texas C.A. 518, 35 S.W. 881 (1896), 85
Turner v. First National Bank of Sulphur Springs, Texas C.A., 234 S.W. 928 (1921), 69
Wilkes v. Adler and Others, 68 Texas 689, 5 S.W. 497 (1887), 59

Virginia

Parrish v. Commonwealth, 81 Virginia 1 (1884), 69, 86

U.S. Supreme Court

Bailey v. Alabama, 219 U.S. 219 (1911), 92
Taylor v. Georgia, 315 U.S. 25 (1942), 92

Northern States

Adams v. McKeeson, 53 Pennsylvania St. 81 (1866), 75
Blake v. Coats, 3 Greene 548 (Iowa 1852), 14
Briggs v. Thompson, 9 Pennsylvania (9 Barr) 338 (1848), 13
Burns v. Cooper, 31 Pennsylvania (7 Casey) 426 (1858), 13
Case v. Hart, 11 Ohio 364 (1842), 15
Doremus v. Howard, 23 New Jersey Law (3 Zal.) 390 (1852), 13–14
Esdon v. Colburn, 28 Vermont (2 Williams) 631 (1856), 15
Figuet v. Allison, 12 Michigan 328 (1864), 14
Fry v. Jones, 2 Rawle (Pennsylvania) 11 (1829), 74
Hurd v. Darling, 16 Vermont 377 (1844), 14
Porter v. Chandler, 27 Minnesota 301 (1880), 75
Ream v. Harnish, 45 Pennsylvania (9 Wright) 376 (1863), 13
Steel v. Frick, 56 Pennsylvania St. 172 (1867), 75

Index

(Cases cited and names of litigants omitted)

Agee, James, 107
Alabama: first postbellum lien law in, 5n; evolution of lien law in, 56–58; abolition of distinction between tenant and cropper in, 74–75; laborer's lien in, 78–79; lien for rent in, 11; peonage in, 91–92
Anti-enticement laws, 90–91, 108
Arkansas: evolution of lien law in, 60–61; laborer's lien in, 78, 79, 80

Black codes, 8, 10, 16, 108

Commission merchants. *See* Factors
Common law, 12, 21, 31, 37, 74
Company towns, 105
Credit: lien laws as means to secure, 4, 7, 8, 9, 10, 15, 103, 108
Crop lien. *See* Liens
Cropper: origins of, 74, 75–76; as a form of wage labor, 66, 104, 105; not a tenant, 68–69, 102–103, 107; abolition of distinction between tenant and cropper in Alabama and North Carolina, 74–75; not a partner, 76–77; litigation concerning status of, 69–73; and forfeiture of wages for abandoning crop, 80–84; legal protection of employers of, 84–86; and right to give lien on future wages, 87–90, 103–104. *See also* Laborer's lien; Anti-enticement laws; Peonage

Factors: antebellum, 7–8, 35–36n, 54–55; postbellum, 28, 29, 35, 38, 40, 54–56
Fields, Barbara J., 109
Florida: first postbellum lien law in, 5n; evolution of lien law in, 58–59
Freedmen's Bureau, 16, 18–20, 22, 23, 25, 32, 37, 76, 78, 93, 110, 114

Gang labor, 15, 25, 66, 76, 110
Georgia: first postbellum lien law in, 5n; evolution of lien law in, 28–45; lien for rent in, 11; laborer's lien in, 32–33, 78, 80–83; peonage in, 91–92; 1868 Constitution of, 33, 78

Johnson, Andrew, 16
Jus dare, jus dicere, 21

Laborer's lien, 77–84, 86, 110. *See also* individual states

123

Landlord-tenant relations: traditional law regarding, 12–14, 65, 93
Lanterns on the Levee, 67, 106, 107
Law: conservatism of, 95–96; ideological function of, 98–99; and relation to politics, 99–101, 111, 114
Let Us Now Praise Famous Men, 107
Liens. *See* individual states, evolution of lien laws in; laborer's lien
Louisiana: first postbellum lien law in, 5n; evolution of lien law in, 54–56; laborer's lien in, 79n

Merchants and storekeepers, antebellum, 8
Merchants, postbellum, 5, 23, 24, 64–65. *See also* individual states, evolution of lien laws in
Mississippi: first postbellum lien law in, 5, 9, 11–12, 24, 46n; lien for rent in, 11–12, 21, 23; evolution of lien law in, 41–42, 45–48; laborer's lien in, 78–79
Mortgage, 18, 23

New Orleans, 54, 55
North Carolina: first postbellum lien law in, 5n, 7; evolution of lien law in, 51–54; laborer's lien in, 80; lien for rent in, 12–15; abolition of distinction between tenant and cropper in, 74

Oklahoma, 86–87

Peonage, 2, 5, 92
Percy, William Alexander, 67–68, 106, 107, 115
Plantation store, 45, 88, 106

Privilege, 54, 55, 79n

Reconstruction, 10, 16, 28, 32, 47, 54, 63, 114
Redeemers, 27, 47, 50, 53, 56, 58, 63, 65, 78, 88, 112, 114

Scrip, 88, 105
Share wages, 15, 66, 93
Sharecropper, 67, 107. *See* Cropper
Sharecropping: and confusion with tenancy, 66n, 105n, 69n, 114
South Carolina: first postbellum lien law in, 5n; evolution of lien law in, 48–51; laborer's lien in, 78, 79, 80; peonage in, 91–92
Stare decisis, 97
Sui juris, 20

Taxes: priority of lien for, 27n
Tenacy: southern similar to northern, 105
Tenant: *See* individual states, evolution of lien laws in; Cropper, not a tenant
Tenant plantations, 105
Tennessee: evolution of lien law in, 61–62; laborer's lien in, 79
Texas: first postbellum lien law in, 5n; evolution of lien law in, 59; laborer's lien in, 79

Virginia: first postbellum lien law in, 60; evolution of lien law in, 60

"Wage slavery," 113
Woodward, C. Vann, 5